Philadelphia Divided

Phila

gave the city a large immigrant population, some 24 percent of the total, but it never rivaled that of New York City, Chicago, or Boston, where up to one-third of the entire population was foreign-born.[9]

Many Philadelphians of Irish descent traced their roots in America back six or seven decades. They initially arrived in enormous numbers: 70,000 of the city's 400,000 residents in 1850 had been born in Ireland. Those numbers, mirroring national trends, tapered off over the years, but as late as 1920 the Irish-born still numbered some 65,000 people or 16 percent of the total foreign-born population. Nineteenth-century Irish immigrants settled in the river wards and took jobs digging canals and laying track for the Pennsylvania Railroad. Luckily for them, they arrived at a moment of economic growth as the city was building its infrastructure and playing a leading role in America's industrial expansion. Although the work was hard, there were many job opportunities in the mid-nineteenth century, and within a generation or two many Irish Americans moved out of South Philadelphia to the streetcar suburbs in the northern and western parts of the city. By the early twentieth century they were generally homeowners and sometimes mid-level managers, the "lace-curtain" Irish as some have called them.[10]

Italian and Jewish immigrants filled homes the Irish had left behind. A small group of Italians had lived in the city since the eighteenth century, but their numbers skyrocketed at the start of the twentieth. In 1870 there were only 500 Italians in Philadelphia, but by 1910 that number had grown to 45,000 and to 65,000 by 1920. Including American-born people of Italian descent, the number of Italian Americans rose to 200,000, or approximately 10 percent of the total population, in that year. Once in the city, Italian immigrants found work at the Pennsylvania Railroad and in the mills, the street cleaning department, and the transit company. Such jobs were a start, but they paid little and seldom led to advancement: one study found that Philadelphia's Italian workers took home only six to nine dollars per week despite working an average of sixty hours. "The Italian people," one immigrant claimed, "were slaves."[11]

Because of their stunted occupational mobility, Italian immigrants had to live in some of the city's worst housing. According to surveys from the period, row houses were so crowded together in Italian South Philadelphia that they blocked out light and fresh air. Investigators called the region "one of the worst housing sections in the country." In one case, thirty families with 123 members lived in just thirty-four rooms. Over the years, Italian immigrants, like the Irish before them, saved money and invested in better housing, and it was not uncommon to find people who lived in their newer homes for fifty years. They took pride in what they owned, comparing it favorably to what their contemporaries had back in Italy. But on the whole, Italians found themselves stigmatized as an undesirable group, unfit for the "respectable" old-stock sections of the city. Italians had to display "conspicuous affluence," one commentator wrote, "to be able to settle in a part of the city not already occupied by Italians or other minorities discriminated against." When an Italian family did stray into Irish or German territory, he continued, they were "repulsed."[12]

Just as jobs and housing failed to unite the Italians and Irish, so too did their Roman Catholicism, and this failure showed that Philadelphia was divided not only along racial lines. The Irish had dominated the church for a century and were ambivalent at best about sharing power with the Italians. Although the Irish recognized that bringing two hundred thousand Italian Catholics into the fold could bolster the church in a city known for its Protestantism and, sometimes, its nativism, they now thought of themselves as respectable members of the community. Forming an alliance with darker-skinned, working-class Italians from the slums would remind the city's Protestants, not to mention the Irish themselves, of their origins. In addition, the Italians practiced a much more public, emotional brand of Catholicism that many Irish found embarrassing. All of this led the Irish to take up the challenge of "Americanizing" the Italian immigrants. Under the leadership of Cardinal Dennis Dougherty and other clergymen, the church established fifteen Italian parishes by the end of the 1920s. Staffed by conservative Irish priests, these churches discouraged Italians from staging religious pageants and urged parishioners to send their children to Catholic schools where Irish priests and nuns could instruct them in "proper" behavior. Many Italians resented this paternalistic attitude, which made them feel that they were "strangers and inferiors" in an "Irish church." As late as the 1970s, elderly Italian Catholics still recalled the Irish clergy of the early twentieth century with a sardonic smile.[13]

Jewish immigrants increased the diversity and divisions in turn-of-the-century Philadelphia. Like the Italians, a small Jewish population had lived in Philadelphia for over a century, establishing one of America's first synagogues, Mikveh Israel, in 1782. With the exception of a small enclave of Eastern Europeans in Port Richmond to the city's northeast, they were overwhelmingly German Jews (from western and central Europe) who practiced their religion quietly, spoke English well, and conformed to the general norms of the community. Then, in 1882, a mass immigration of Eastern European Jews (all called Russian Jews, whatever their origins) began. Touched off by an 1881 Russian pogrom, it brought some two million Jews to America over the next thirty years. Most went to New York City, but a substantial number landed in Philadelphia and Boston. By 1920 some 95,000 foreign-born Jews called Philadelphia home, with another 100,000 having been born in the city. Jews, like the Italians, made up about 10 percent of the total population.[14]

Philadelphia's Jewish population, despite a few successful German Jewish businessmen, was overwhelmingly working class. New arrivals for the most part shunned heavy labor, instead becoming peddlers and garment workers. Jewish women constituted about one-half of all workers in the needle trades in a city that produced 5 percent of the nation's textiles, and they found their workplace conditions abominable. "Intolerable filth, pestilence and disease" made these shops "the worst . . . of any city in the trade," Charles Reichers, general secretary of the United Garment Workers, told Congress. Such conditions fed a radical, or at least working-class, politics. Many immigrants, particularly labor leaders, had been exposed to socialism in Eastern Europe and used that experience to push for political and shop-floor unity. Working-class Jews, one study found, made up the bulk of the city's Communist Party (CP). Jews also played a leading role in the city's two garment workers' unions, the International Ladies Garment Workers Union (ILGWU) and the Amalgamated Clothing Workers of America (ACWA), which staged the first major strikes in the city's needle trades and established the leftist militancy that many working-class Jews adopted. As they built the garment industry unions, Jewish leaders knew that a strictly Jewish movement would fail. Italians and African American women constituted a large minority of the workforce, and Jews built alliances with them. The ACWA relied on organizers named Morriconi and Palermo to attract Italian workers, and one scholar of Philadelphia's sweatshops commented that Italians and Jews "developed a kinship . . . far above any other immigrant groups." Likewise, the ILGWU supported black organizing efforts and developed programs to bring in more African American members. The alliance of Jews, Italians, and African Americans in the garment workers unions hinted at the cross-race connections that could be made among working-class Philadelphians, but in the 1920s such relationships were rare.[15]

As members of immigrant groups moved through the river wards and established their own niches within the city's job market, they often led insular lives. Irish, Italian, and Jewish Philadelphians lived in circumscribed neighborhoods and often worked at jobs that offered them only limited contact with other working-class Philadelphians. To be sure, the ILGWU and

ACWA demonstrated that different peoples could work together, but overall the story was one of divisions that show the limitations of thinking in terms of a monolithic "white" community in 1920s' Philadelphia. Many European immigrants were still arriving in the early twentieth century and creating their own places in the housing and job markets. These were not established "white" communities that blacks "invaded" during the Great Migration; they were, instead, ethnically fluid arenas that African Americans tried to fit into. In other words, ethnicity had not yet completely "flattened into race," in the historian John McGreevy's term. But the arrival of tens of thousands of African Americans pushed race closer and closer to the fore, and in the ensuing years color, much more than ethnicity, became the dividing line in Philadelphia.[16]

Black–Euro-American Relations

As African Americans gained resources they tried to move out of the slums and into adjoining neighborhoods. Old-stock groups reacted by moving or by fighting to "preserve" their communities. The Germans and the Irish in North and West Philadelphia had lived in the country long enough to accumulate the resources necessary to buy homes in the suburbs, and they were the first to go: fifty thousand people moved to neighborhoods adjoining the city or to new suburbs in the surrounding counties as the area's black population doubled. Sadie Mossell was astounded by the rapid changes in parts of North Philadelphia, writing that, by 1919 in some areas, "one could scarcely find a white family." Germantown and parts of North and West Philadelphia went through what would only later be called "white flight." Some Philadelphians turned to violence to keep blacks out of their neighborhoods. The worst such rioting occurred in the summer of 1918 when African Americans moved into homes bordering South Philadelphia's black district. One woman became so fearful after a mob threw a rock through her window that she fired a revolver to summon the police. The lone policeman who responded could not quiet the crowd and had to turn in a riot call to get enough officers to break up the mob. A near lynching took place downtown the next day, after which violence flickered across the city for the rest of the week. The *Philadelphia Tribune*, the city's leading black newspaper, told African Americans to stand their ground and "burn [the rioters'] hides with any weapon that comes handy." The perpetrators, the paper tellingly added, "represent the scum of Erin's sod." That at least some of the aggressors were Irish surprised few blacks, who told city authorities, "The people with the most prejudice . . . seem to be the Irish."[17]

The rise of the Ku Klux Klan further demonstrated the antiblack violence of the era. By its peak in the mid-1920s, some three hundred thousand members had joined the Pennsylvania KKK, which was, in the words of one scholar, "the most important 'realm' in the Klan's so-called 'Domain of the Northeast.'" Philadelphia was the center of Klan activity in the state with twenty klaverns, including those in Germantown, West Philadelphia, Strawberry Mansion, and suburban Montgomery and Delaware counties. In some ways Pennsylvania's Klan was as disturbed by cultural change and Catholicism as it was by African Americans. "What is the Ku Klux Klan's next great battle?" one KKK leader rhetorically asked in 1927. "The battle to prevent the Roman hierarchy from seating Mr. Al Smith in the presidential chair," he responded. Irish Catholics, for obvious reasons, gave the Klan no support, but it was still an important tool that other old-stock whites used to intimidate blacks. The Klan burned a cross in Haverford in 1924 to "frighten the Negroes and others out of the section." It committed one of the few lynchings in state history when it killed a black man in Beaver, Pennsylvania. And, in September 1923, Philadelphia Klansmen broke into a house owned by two black nurses on Cumberland Street and "broke the windows, disconnected the bath tub, turned on the water in the house, [and] wrote K.K.K. on the wall and woodwork." Despite its strength in numbers, the Klan lost momentum by the late 1920s as the city's racial and ethnic relations briefly calmed and turmoil within the Klan's leadership wracked the organization. But while the Klan withered, the attitudes that produced it did not. "There was nothing wrong with the Klan principles," one ex-member recalled. "But the members—they weren't big enough for the Order." Over the next fifteen years, other right-wing groups—the Bund, the Black Shirts, and others—took the Klan's place, but the KKK was merely dormant, not dead. In the immediate post–World War II years the Klan reemerged, this time focusing its wrath almost exclusively on blacks.[18]

While old-stock Philadelphians often responded by fleeing or fighting, the newest immigrants had no such choice. Many Russian Jews in the early 1920s still earned low wages and lived in some of the city's worst housing. A 1921 Housing Association report found that only 28.6 percent of Jews lived in homes "equipped for sanitation, convenience and comfort." This number far exceeded the black rate of 10.5 percent but was well below old-stock numbers. Many Jews, in fact, lived side by side with blacks and felt a certain kinship with their neighbors, the sense that they shared ties forged in oppression. Jews, like blacks, often faced violence when they crossed into Irish neighborhoods. Sixty years after the fact, elderly Jews still pointed to

Many white Philadelphians found the arrival of thousands of black migrants threatening. While some whites moved to the suburbs, others joined the Ku Klux Klan to "protect" their neighborhoods. Here the Klan marches in Frankford, 1927. Courtesy of Temple University Libraries, Urban Archives, Philadelphia PA.

"attacks by Irish American children on the way to school" as their most vivid memories. National events contributed to this feeling too. From the Leo Frank lynching to school and workplace discrimination to nasty portrayals in popular culture, Jews argued that they faced much the same prejudice as African Americans.[19]

Some Jews acted on their beliefs, building liberal and left-wing organizations with blacks. Joel Spingarn, Henry Moskowitz, and other Jewish leaders, for example, helped found the National Association for the Advancement of Colored People (NAACP). In Philadelphia, Rabbi Eli Mayer sat on the NAACP branch's board of directors, and Jacob Billikopf of the Federation of Jewish Charities raised money for the association. More radical Jews

Members of the Klan's Kamp No. 1 in Philadelphia, 1927.
Courtesy of Temple University Libraries, Urban Archives, Philadelphia PA.

recruited blacks into the ILGWU and the CP, where some African Americans reached the highest ranks. Thomas Nabried, who joined in 1928, attended school in Moscow and then worked as an organizer all over the city as well as in Bucks County. In his talks, Nabried pressed the "necessity for equality between the black and white races in this country, if Communism is to succeed." He eventually rose to be the party's city chairman, from 1942 to 1945, and then served as district chairman for eastern Pennsylvania and Delaware until his death in 1965. The CP showed the possibility of an interracial alliance in Philadelphia made up chiefly of left-leaning Jews and African Americans.[20]

Black-Jewish relations were hardly perfect, however. A number of scholars have analyzed the relationship's problems, pointing out that Jewish leaders "played with the issues of racism and black status as a way of working out [their own] problems." Battling racism, in Hasia Diner's words, let Jews "prove how American they had become [by] quoting the Constitution and other documents of the American creed." Jews, in this view, supported black rights out of both honest concern and a subconscious desire for their own advancement, primarily through acculturation. In Philadelphia, the tension between Jewish aspirations and the desire for friendly relations with blacks frequently emerged. Jewish leaders of the Communist Party often took a paternalistic stance because blacks were supposedly not as politically advanced. Jews, who owned many small shops in black Philadelphia, swore they treated their customers with complete fairness, but blacks found that while their business was welcome, they could not work in many of those stores. Likewise, some Jews bought property in black neighborhoods, and their landlord status raised thorny problems. A writer in the *Philadelphia Tribune* called Jews "'dollar crazy' people who were always prepared to invade black communities." Philadelphia was not the "hotbed of Negro anti-Semitism" as some suggested, but certainly there were tensions in the relationship. Still, more issues united blacks and Jews than separated them, and they formed at worst an uneasy alliance and at best the core of progressive politics in the city over the next few decades.[21]

The relationship between Italians and the black newcomers likewise was uneven. Italians also faced discrimination at the hands of old-stock Philadelphians and resented their second-class status. Nothing infuriated them more than newspapers such as the *Philadelphia Inquirer* asking, "Are we becoming a mongrel nation?" Pervasive bigoted views meant Italian immigrants had little opportunity (not to mention wherewithal) to move to the old-stock suburbs. Instead, they solidified their presence in South Philadelphia, often buying property from African Americans and settling in as neighbors. Some affinity between the two groups did develop: African Americans told city investigators that, compared to the Irish, "The Italians seem to be tolerant." But men like Toney Pecoro, who led the angry mob to the Henrys' home, showed that many Italians were not so open-minded. As Italian Americans bought homes in South Philadelphia, they became more rooted in the neighborhood than were the Irish and Jewish residents. Many Irish Philadelphians had the money to live in other areas of the city, and many Jews rented, rather than owned, their homes. Also, it was feasible for either group to move to the city's periphery if they felt overwhelmed by racial change. Italian families early in the twentieth century owned some two-thirds of the homes in their section of South Philadelphia. They bought there, in part, because their work for the city's sanitation and road construction crews required them to go to different parts of the city each day, and their central location in South Philadelphia gave them easier access to their jobs. This residential pattern, tied to workplace needs, mirrored that of other groups, such as the Poles, who lived near the city's heavy industrial plants, and some Irish, who bought near Kensington's textile mills. Religion too played a part in Italian rootedness, as the Catholic hierarchy encouraged Italians to build expensive churches and schools in their "national" parishes. Bound by a heavy investment in their parish's infrastructure and having limited financial resources, few Italians could move. Because they were tied to their neighborhoods, Italians in Philadelphia often reacted to black newcomers with intolerance.[22]

As fractured as Philadelphia was in its housing market, the job market was just as bad. Here, the fault line lay even more clearly along the racial divide. By the 1920s, Irish, Italian, and Jewish Philadelphians had distributed themselves into various workplace niches depending on such variables as their time of arrival in America, their skill sets, and their employers' prejudices. Italians were hardly happy being on the labor market's lowest rungs, but at least they had relatively secure employment. Like the Irish and to a lesser extent the Jews, they wanted no workplace competition from blacks. Thus African Americans found almost all routes to advancement closed.[23]

World War I opened some opportunities but only temporarily. With the onset of the war and the concurrent end of European immigration, Philadelphia employers, including the Pennsylvania Railroad, Westinghouse, and Midvale Steel, turned to the South for cheap labor. Midvale, under the direction of Frederick Winslow Taylor, had hired blacks for decades, mainly to cut down on worker solidarity, and was the only business with a history of employing black workers. The others did so because of the war. Regardless of their motives, these Philadelphia companies and others took on unprecedented numbers of black workers, some 33,500 in all. The close of hostilities ended many of these opportunities. As companies lost government contracts and laid off workers, blacks faced the familiar problem of being "last hired, first fired." Unemployment in black Philadelphia quickly exceeded prewar levels, and the continued arrival of migrants only worsened conditions. Many firms refused to hire blacks at all, with Budd, Bendix, Cramps Shipyard, and Baldwin Locomotive employing 35,000 people but zero blacks until the late 1930s. The city's textile mills, with 45,000 workers, employed only 280 African Americans, all janitors. And politicians gave blacks only 800 of the city's 25,000 jobs. Most employers offered little indication of ever relenting: one study found four-fifths of job orders specified "whites only," and another found that about half of those surveyed did not want to hire blacks because, they said, their company would have to build separate facilities to appease their white workers. Their World War I employment gains having disappeared, for the next fifteen years African Americans found few opportunities open to them beyond domestic service and unskilled labor.[24]

White workers, particularly union members who had at least a little say in the workplace, helped to create this discriminatory environment. Philadelphia, with its smaller industries and highly skilled workforce, was a craft union, AFL (American Federation of Labor) town with little history of industrial unionism. Across the nation AFL unions were notorious for their segregated locals, and Philadelphia was no different: a 1910 study of several Philadelphia industries found that of 63,000 unionized workers, only 200 were black. AFL union members protested vehemently whenever the textile mills and shipbuilding firms they worked for suggested hiring blacks. To be sure, the ILGWU pushed for integration in some garment shops, and the Industrial Workers of the World (IWW) established an interracial union on the docks in the 1910s and 1920s, but these were rare exceptions that proved the rule.[25]

It is important, however, not to overemphasize union discrimination. At no time before the 1930s, as Walter Licht noted in his study of Philadelphia's laborers, did unionization rates top 10 percent. For years employers across Pennsylvania had used state and private police as well as court injunctions to intimidate workers and to break their unions. "You can't run a coalmine," businessman Richard Mellon once said, "without machine guns." Philadelphia employers of the late teens and 1920s may not have turned to violence as readily as Mellon, but they eagerly participated in a national offensive to

African Americans, such as these hod carriers in 1924, generally found limited job prospects. Most worked in manual labor with little chance to advance to skilled positions. Courtesy of Temple University Libraries, Urban Archives, Philadelphia PA.

roll back labor's wartime gains. In textiles, where the trend toward hard-wood floors and shorter skirts had already hurt business, employers brought further pressure to bear by cutting wages, firing union members, and establishing the open shop. At the Pennsylvania Railroad, management broke a strike to gain control of wage rates in 1922–23. Workers in the tight postwar economy feared fighting back too strongly because, beyond the threat of physical violence, they knew that many workers had lost their jobs. Cramp's Shipyard was foundering and about to close, several textile mills had moved to the South, and metal manufacturing seemed to be in an irreversible decline. By the late 1920s, workers of European descent faced uncertain employment prospects at best. Wage rates were falling, security was waning, and unions offered little support. Small wonder they generally regarded blacks as dangerous competitors rather than potential allies.[26]

The Great Depression only exacerbated these problems. The highest level of unemployment hit the already depressed textile industry and accounted for some 15 percent of all the city's jobless workers. All told, some one hundred thousand mill hands lost their jobs in the first three years of the Depression, and it took them an average of thirty-seven weeks to find work again. With jobs so scarce, many immigrants and their descendants, who took such pride in owning their homes, faced foreclosure. Between 1928 and 1933 the city auctioned off more than ninety thousand homes. Black unemployment, which stood at 24 percent in supposedly prosperous 1927, climbed as high as 61 percent over the next few years. In some districts government officials found blacks unemployed at rates four times higher than those of their white neighbors. The Armstrong Association (Philadelphia's version of the Urban League), which took pride in its ability to place black job seekers, reported that even after the worst of the Depression had passed the association had secured work for only an anemic 3.9 percent of its applicants. More worrisome were the cases of starvation turning up in Philadelphia hospitals. One man testified to Congress that Philadelphians were getting so desperate to eat that they had to scavenge "like hogs for scraps of fruit and vegetables littering the city's waterfront."[27]

Politics

City politicians, all Republicans, offered little hope of solving these myriad problems. The GOP had two overlapping camps, the first comprising big businessmen and their conservative political allies. Joseph Pew of the Sun Oil Company, Joseph Grundy and G. Mason Owlett of the Pennsylvania Manufacturers' Association (PMA), and others dominated this wing. They held a Gilded Age view of government that limited public authority to establishing the rules of the marketplace, making internal improvements, and letting laissez-faire economics flow unfettered. To them, anything that interfered with business would bring the entire state "tumbling down in ruins." These corporate leaders put their money to work in politics. One commentator referred to Pew as "the chief Republican angel of modern times" for his contributions to the party. Such men saw little need for government to provide security for workers, be they of European or African descent. These businessmen found their champion in Philadelphia mayor J. Hampton Moore, who held the office in 1920–23 and 1932–35. Before becoming mayor,

Moore had served several terms in the U.S. Congress, where he always argued that there was little need for state power. "The government," he said, "should build canals, move commerce, keep the protective tariff, preserve the peace, and keep costs to a minimum." In Philadelphia, Moore refused to change his thinking about government relief. "I toured the lower sections of South Philadelphia," he said in 1931. "I went into the small streets and saw little of poverty. . . . There is no starvation in Philadelphia." The people, he claimed, were "merely living within their means."[28]

The Vare political machine dominated the Republican Party's other faction. William Vare and his brothers had grown up on a pig farm in South Philadelphia and made their first fortune on a municipal contract to collect garbage. Early on they learned the value of access to government work, which brought them into politics. By World War I, the Vares were consolidating South Philadelphia's wards into a unit that would send them and their allies to both the statehouse and the Congress and allow them to control local government for the next twenty years. Ward leaders and municipal employees formed the machine's bedrock. They showed utter loyalty to Vare and did anything necessary to turn out the Republican vote. "My platform is short, sweet, and easy to say," Freddie Lunt, a ward leader, told anyone who asked. "I am for William S. Vare." Throughout the city, anyone with a government job paid deference, and more, to the Vares. One study found that some 94 percent of city employees paid an "assessment" to the Republican Party and that those who failed to contribute were summoned to their ward's headquarters. The Vares sometimes turned to even dirtier methods of maintaining their rule. They had Democratic poll watchers beaten up and jailed; they handed immigrants two dollars and a ballot as they entered the polling station; and they registered the dead, the "cemetery vote" they called it. The journalist John Gunther probably was right to describe Philadelphia as "the most smearily corrupt city in America."[29]

The Vares had more than corruption and dubious ballot box activities going for them in making Philadelphia a Republican stronghold. Voting Republican had become a habit for Pennsylvanians since the Civil War. From 1893 to 1931, Democrats lost ninety-five of ninety-six statewide elections—one Democratic gubernatorial candidate withdrew to run instead for Grand Exalted Ruler of the Elks. While residents of other northern cities turned to the Democratic Party during the Depression, Mayor Moore took office after winning over 90 percent of the vote in November 1931. Even if the Democrats had been a viable option, the city's Euro- and African Americans demonstrated little desire to leave the Republican Party, as they knew that supporting the Vares brought real, if limited, benefits. Poor Jews, African Americans, and others could find ward heelers to intercede with the courts and get them food and clothing when needed, and heelers only helped Republicans. Italians and African Americans consequently gave Vare candidates 90 percent of their vote in most elections. The Republicans' historic connection to Abraham Lincoln, not to mention African Americans' experience with the Democratic Party of the South, cemented black loyalty. The Vares did not build some sort of multicultural coalition based on equality for all—blacks, Italians, and Jews knew they would never win important nominations or get more prestigious city hall jobs—but with no other party in town, these Philadelphians took what they could get from local politics.[30]

Philadelphia in the first three decades of the twentieth century, then, was dominated by a Republican Party that contained an odd assortment of people and interests. Big businessmen and old-stock, rugged individualists rubbed shoulders with Jews, blacks, Italians, the Irish, and their patrons, the pig-farming Vares. For the most part, businessmen contented themselves with life on the Main Line and paid more attention to state and national politics than to the internal workings of the city. The Vares maintained an unspoken agreement with corporate interests: the machine would be allowed to run the city without interference, and, in return, the machine would make sure that congressmen and senators who would vote for a high tariff and limited government intervention in the economy got elected.[31]

Cracks in the system did appear, most notably with Al Smith's 1928 run for the presidency. In that election, Smith was the first candidate to address the concerns of immigrant voters, and they supported him across the nation. In Philadelphia, the Irish, the Jews, and the Italians were all drawn to the first presidential candidate who spoke to their interests. African Americans were the only group that offered Smith little support, giving him only 23 percent of their vote. To some scholars, this election betokened a later New Deal coalition, but during the 1930 U.S. Senate election, all of these groups in Philadelphia settled back into their Republican voting habits. Years of casting Republican ballots, combined with the power of the Vare machine, meant that Philadelphians would not easily leave the Republican Party.[32]

The Depression, more than the Smith campaign, altered Philadelphia politics as new Democratic Party leaders emerged to offer an alternative to the Republicans. One of the most important of these leaders was Joseph Guffey, who hailed from Pittsburgh and had been a Democratic leader for years. This meant little until the 1930s, as in 1929 his home city had only five thousand registered Democrats in a voting population of one hundred and seventy-five

TABLE I

Percentages of Selected Ethnic Groups Voting Democratic, 1924–32

	1924 (President)	1928 (President)	1930 (Senator)	1932 (President)
Irish	20	68	31	55
Italian	8	61	25	51
Jewish	7	48	16	50
Black	6	23	9	27

Sources: Voting data drawn from Shover, "Ethnicity and Religion in Philadelphia Politics"; Shover, "Emergence of a Two-Party System"; Grove, "Decline of the Republican Machine"; Miller, "Negro in Pennsylvania Politics"; Maiale, "Italian Vote in Philadelphia"; Greenberg, "Philadelphia Democratic Party."

Note: Since Philadelphia never compiled voting statistics by race or ethnicity in this period, these data rely on the work of the scholars listed above, and an elaborate method pioneered by John Shover was used to tabulate the electoral results. For a detailed discussion of this method, which uses census manuscripts, registration records, and district maps to reconstruct the city's voting patterns, see Wolfinger, "Rise and Fall," chap. 1.

thousand. But early on Guffey recognized Franklin Roosevelt's potential and gave his full support to the New York governor. When Roosevelt took office, he thanked Guffey by giving him control of most of the federal jobs in Pennsylvania, and Guffey used his patronage powers to build allegiance to the Democratic Party.[33]

Part of that allegiance came from black Pennsylvanians. In the summer of 1932, Robert Vann, editor of the influential black newspaper the *Pittsburgh Courier*, visited Guffey and stunned the Democratic leader by denouncing the Republicans for "cashing in for seventy years on the debt of the Civil War, without really doing anything further for colored people." Guffey then persuaded Roosevelt to create a black division in the Democratic Campaign Committee with Vann at the head. With this support from the Democrats, Vann famously advised blacks to "go turn Lincoln's picture to the wall. That debt has been paid in full." Although a majority of Philadelphia's African Americans did not move to the Democratic Party in 1932, Vann's public support of the Democrats assured blacks that they could legitimately cast their vote for Roosevelt.[34]

Newspapers also played a major role in making the Democrats a viable party. J. David Stern, a man of Jewish ancestry with long but intermittent ties to Philadelphia, used his *Philadelphia Record* to support Roosevelt in 1932. The African American editor J. Max Barber also boosted FDR by using his *Independent* to question black allegiance to the GOP. "There exists no sound reason why the Negro should be permanently wedded to the Republican Party," he told his readers. "We advise Negroes everywhere to give their votes to that party which is willing to give you most for them. . . . They want votes and you want patronage, rights, and privileges. It is purely a business proposition." E. Washington Rhodes, publisher of the *Tribune* and the city's leading black Republican, was more skeptical than Barber about the Democrats. A southern migrant, Rhodes always pointed to the South as the home of the Democratic Party and argued that the selection of John Nance Garner, Roosevelt's Texan running mate, spoke volumes about the presidential candidate. "The best way out for the Negro," Rhodes wrote, is "to support the Republican." But having a viable Democratic Party, he acknowledged, would help the city's blacks because both parties would have to "do more than make empty promises." With as staunch a Republican as Rhodes talking about the benefits of a Democratic Party, Philadelphia's politics were clearly in flux.[35]

The Republican machine held on in 1932, but barely. Of all the immigrant groups, the Irish and Italians provided Roosevelt with the highest levels of support, 55 and 51 percent, respectively. Jews gave him about 50 percent, blacks only 27 percent of their vote. Vare ended up holding the city for the Republicans but only by 70,000 votes, a slender victory compared to previous elections. Likewise, the state stayed Republican by a total of only 157,000 votes. Of the five states that Hoover carried, Pennsylvania was by far the largest, but it was no grand victory for the Republicans. Pittsburgh went Democratic for the first time since 1856, Hoover received 600,000 fewer votes statewide than in 1928, and Philadelphia, which usually gave at least three-quarters of its vote to the Republicans, now seemed up for grabs. The Democrats were not yet a force in Philadelphia, but they were becoming viable.[36]

Compared to most other cities and states, support for Roosevelt in Pennsylvania in 1932 was unimpressive, but in the context of Philadelphia as a Republican stronghold controlled by an entrenched political machine and corporate interests, the 1932 election offered a glimmer of what was to come in the mid-1930s. A tenuous coalition had begun to form. But despite the fact that more ordinary Philadelphians had voted Democratic than ever before, the coalition was still weak: African Americans had not really joined the other working-class groups at the ballot box, and none had offered the Democratic nominee its overwhelming support. Outside the voting booth, the alliance was even shakier. Philadelphians of Irish, Italian, and Eastern European descent, having scrambled for jobs and housing in the city for decades, often placed little trust in one another, and the huge number of black migrants arriving in the teens and 1920s only exacerbated these tensions. Whether in municipal employment, the work gangs of the Pennsylvania Railroad, or the neighborhoods of working-class Philadelphia, different ethnic groups regarded one another with suspicion. Overcoming that suspicion —bridging the differences between the peoples of Philadelphia—was the often overwhelming job of the Democratic Party. There were occasional moments of solidarity, as when Jews, blacks, and Italians came together in the ILGWU or the Communist Party, but those moments were rare. Over the next decade the Democrats struggled, and sometimes managed, to pull a coalition together, but it was always an unstable alliance whose constituents seldom agreed on anything more than voting for FDR.

The Rise of New Deal Liberalism

This defeat of Governor Landon . . . is as dangerous as a revolution.
—Philadelphia Republican, 1936

It looked like Mardi Gras in Philadelphia as half a million people joined or just watched the parade in Center City. Bands and drum corps marched through the streets, belting out "Happy Days Are Here Again." Throngs of people, ecstatic despite the cold November weather, surged through the heart of the city singing, dancing, and laughing. Some rode in horse-and-buggies to signify that the old days were gone while others carried coffins with effigies of Alf Landon, J. P. Morgan, and the DuPonts. A solemn bugler played taps for the Republican Party. The crowds lingered on Broad Street, at the Union League, cheering President Roosevelt in front of the giant brick-and-brownstone building that embodied Philadelphia conservatism. The crowd parted for just a moment to allow a young man with a broom to industriously sweep the thoroughfare; 1936 was indeed a clean sweep for the Democratic Party.[1]

In Reyburn Plaza and around city hall, hundreds of thousands of Philadelphians were enraptured by the city's Democratic leaders. Torches lit the night as party officials marched through the streets, shaking hands and congratulating each other on ending seven decades of Republican rule. Some called for Pennsylvania governor George Earle to succeed FDR in 1940. Others carried signs urging "Kelly for Mayor." Jack Kelly, the head of Philadelphia's Democratic Party, held his hand up to that one and gave his supporters a huge grin. To Kelly this was even better than six nights earlier, the day of FDR's sweeping victory, when he and other local Democrats had led a throng of 15,000 people to the Union League to celebrate. There Kelly had climbed the imposing building's facade and gotten in a fistfight with a doorman sporting sunflower buttons in honor of Alf Landon, the Republican candidate. But on this night, one marked by revelry rather than brawls, Kelly could only smile. He had helped carry Philadelphia for the Democrats in a presidential election for the first time since the Civil War era, his comrade in the governor's mansion was enjoying a small boom to run for president in 1940, and thousands of people wanted Kelly to be the city's next mayor. It was, he said, "a great and glorious victory." Liberal politics, from the vantage point of the Union League steps no less, was on the rise, at least for the moment.[2]

Given the Democrats' attempt in the early 1930s to build a multiethnic liberal coalition, it was no accident that as the Irish Kelly surveyed the parade he saw Anna Brancato, Anthony DiSilvestro, and other Italian American politicians leading some groups, Leon Sacks heading a Jewish contingent, and the African American magistrate Ed Henry and others directing the representatives of Philadelphia's black districts. Italians, Jews, African Americans, and the Irish to varying degrees all came together in a coalition whose power reached its greatest height with Roosevelt's reelection in 1936. That coalition did not hold for long, but at the time it indeed must have seemed to Republicans that a revolution had come.[3]

Labor

The political transformation of John B. "Jack" Kelly, who assumed the leadership of the city's Democratic Party in the early 1930s, reveals much about the changes in Philadelphia's politics. The Irish American Kelly, who won national renown as an Olympic gold medalist in rowing, started out as an apprentice bricklayer and kept his union card his entire life. Thanks to his athletic fame and well-known work regimen, Kelly moved out of blue-collar work and started his own brickwork company, which became one of the largest firms in the country. He had only marginal interest in politics, and that was stunted by the Vare machine and mainline WASPs who paid him little attention. Al Smith's 1928 campaign led Kelly to move to the Democratic Party, but until Roosevelt took office in 1932 his shift meant little. The Depression and Roosevelt's programs, combined with Republican inactivity, drove Kelly to get more involved. "Until I saw a bread line for the first time," Kelly remembered, "I stayed out of politics." Kelly brought with him a number of Irish American lawyers and businessmen who bolstered the moribund Democratic Party with their energy and enthusiasm. Because of their heritage, these men had been unable to find a place in the Republican leadership, but the Democrats welcomed them. Jewish leaders, such as the banker and real estate investor Albert Greenfield and publisher J. David Stern, had experienced the same kind of discrimination. Collectively they forged a Democratic team that sought to appeal to the city's ethnic populations.[4]

Stoking liberal political activism in a city dominated for a century by Republicanism was easier said than done. Top Democrats found Philadelphia's progressive politics stunted by decades of big business conservatism and political machine control. Until the 1930s, unions had played only a small role in the city, the Communist Party had faced constant repression, and the GOP had controlled local patronage. But all of this changed as the Depression and the resulting New Deal inspired thousands to get involved in left/liberal politics. This is not to say that ordinary Philadelphians supported the Democratic Party unquestioningly or automatically united on most issues, but they did live in an atmosphere conducive to political activism that helped the Democrats create a coalition.

Organized labor was one of the key building blocks of Democratic politics, but unions were weak institutions when the Depression began. The struggle to build a politically active, progressive union movement demonstrated the difficulty Philadelphians had in overcoming internecine labor conflicts and the power of local corporations. In the late 1920s, the AFL dominated Philadelphia's unions. They practiced a conservative politics, accepting city leaders' pervasive belief in laissez-faire capitalism. A. J. Muste, a former minister and leader at Brookwood Labor College, grew so disgusted with the AFL that he formed a chapter of the Conference of Progressive Labor Action to push a more socialist agenda in the city, but it made little headway. The Depression forced the AFL to alter its cautious tactics and demand help from the government, with the national AFL's William Green in particular coming to realize the need for federal intervention and massive assistance to the unemployed. Local leaders, such as Adolph Hirschberg of the Central Labor Union (the AFL's umbrella organization in the city) and Lewis Hines, Philadelphia's head AFL organizer, followed Green's lead and demanded that the government stop foreclosures of private homes, prevent utility companies from turning off service, and provide $100 million in direct relief. By the mid-1930s the Central Labor Union had become such a strong advocate for working-class Philadelphians that it claimed nearly a quarter of a million members.[5]

The emergence of the Congress of Industrial Organizations (CIO) added momentum to the labor activism begun by the AFL. Established by John L. Lewis in 1935, the CIO practiced an industrial unionism that accepted all workers in an industry regardless of their specific jobs. Members rejected the AFL's craft unionism based on organizing members according to their trades. In the CIO's eyes, the AFL's philosophy divided workers instead of uniting them and made it more difficult to organize workers in the nation's growing heavy industries with their multiplicity of less-skilled jobs performed by many different racial and ethnic groups. Industrial unionism, with its emphasis on the common needs of all workers, swept the nation's manufacturing plants in the mid- to late 1930s, winning victories in auto, steel, rubber, and other industries. Not that it was easy: CIO organizers faced bitter opposition in Detroit, Chicago, and Philadelphia.[6]

Many Philadelphia companies faced militant unionism for the first time when the CIO came to town. A decade earlier the radical Industrial Workers of the World had organized Philadelphia's docks, but its efforts largely failed to spread to other industries. The CIO, however, brought waves of determined organizers who implemented a systematic campaign. Just as important as sheer determination was the context provided by the New Deal. With the National Labor Relations Act of 1935 (also known as the Wagner Act) in place, the CIO had federal assurance that workers had the right to form unions and to participate in collective bargaining. CIO organizers swept into the city with at least tacit federal support and immediately started signing up workers at Baldwin Locomotive, Midvale Steel, Apex Hosiery, Electric Storage Battery (Exide), and a host of other companies.[7]

Most owners refused to accept worker organizing and turned to friendly Republican judges and politicians to implement lockouts, file injunctions, and instigate violence. The most notorious case took place before the CIO arrived, but it set the pattern for what the organization would face and helped prepare workers in the city to accept a militant union message. At H. C. Aberle's mill in Kensington, hundreds of textile workers had joined the American Federation of Full Fashioned Hosiery Workers and walked out in 1930 to force the company to stabilize their wage rates and recognize their union. Aberle ignored them and hired strikebreakers to run his plant. Sympathetic judges ruled that the replacement workers had the right to carry guns and issued injunctions to keep the strikers out of the way. The workers seethed. Milling around in front of the plant, they attacked some of the scabs. The police immediately moved in and arrested sixty-five strikers, which heightened tensions. Later that night, a carload of strikebreakers left the mill, and several strikers pursued them. When the first car stopped, the unionists rushed at them, and three strikers were shot. Carl Mackley died of his wounds, and Kensington erupted in anger. The mayor had to send in five hundred police to calm the community.[8]

Such events united the city's workers and made them more militant. Adopting a strategy that worked to greatest effect at General Motors' facilities in Michigan, in 1937 Philadelphia workers used the sit-down strike to take over Exide and several textile mills. Rather than march in the street, workers who engaged in these sit-down strikes took over the plants, threw out management and their guards, barricaded themselves inside the buildings, and dared the owners to remove them with force. Companies were reluctant to use their traditional head-cracking methods because in the midst of the Depression many working-class people sympathized with the strikers, and violent tactics could lead to massive rioting. With the workers in the plant, moreover, hundreds of thousands of dollars worth of equipment was in harm's way. Also, managers knew they were operating in a new political atmosphere in the state. "I give you my solemn pledge," Democratic governor Earle told an assembled group of unionists, "that so long as I am governor of Pennsylvania the police power of this Commonwealth will never be used to limit or destroy the rights of unionization." Given the circumstances, many of Philadelphia's staunchest antiunion companies gave in to the demands of their workers. As the CIO swept through the city's plants, the union movement looked unstoppable.[9]

The mid-1930s represented the apex of working-class power and unity in the city. The AFL's Central Labor Union, which had always treated other unions as dangerous rivals, reached an uneasy truce with the CIO, and together they formed a massive front of several hundred thousand workers. Organized labor's greatest strength was in the clothing and textile industries where the ACWA and ILGWU had over twenty thousand members, but the manufacturing industry, led by Westinghouse, Philco, Budd, and others, was also the site of mass organizing. All told, some two-thirds of Philadelphia's workers had union contracts by the 1940s, and according to one study, that number swelled to 90 percent for production line workers. Labor leaders built their unions in part by offering activities that connected people's home and work lives. The theater district had vibrant working-class playhouses that staged the works of Clifford Odets. Unions sponsored sports leagues, picnics, and dances to further working-class solidarity. At companies such as Philco and Disston, unions published journals to inform members of important events and to urge them to support their locals. And workers' children attended educational programs that taught about "peace, economic justice, racial understanding . . . [and] the nature of capitalist society." The Catholic Church got involved too, opening labor schools for the benefit of Irish, Italian, and Eastern European workers. As working-class people came together to play, attend the theater, and go to school, they began to recognize their common interests and forged an extra-workplace solidarity. Working-class Philadelphians, for the first time in memory, joined together on their shop floors and in their union halls and neighborhoods.[10]

Unity was an essential first step, but labor leaders wanted to convert solidarity into political power. As ACWA leader Charles Weinstein told his members, unions had to engage in politics because "only by Government Legislation will the working class as a whole benefit." Unions developed an array of strategies to politicize their members. At Philco, Disston, and elsewhere, locals published journals that carried the usual birth and marriage announcements but also analyzed the Wagner Act, the possibility of forming a Labor Party, and problems in the banking system and stock market. Unions made sure to get women involved, a particularly important move given the city's numerous clothing and textile industries. The ACWA and other unions held regular "women's only" meetings where speakers discussed cooking and fashion but also urged women to engage in formal politics and to take an active part in their locals. And women did just that, conducting voter registration drives, ushering at political rallies, and distributing literature in support of FDR. Union-inspired activism spread to people's neighborhoods too. In the Mackley Homes, named after the murdered Carl Mackley, union members established a legislative committee and hosted lectures on socialized medicine and other political topics. Elsewhere, workers staged debates on unemployment and organized letter-writing campaigns designed to persuade their legislators to support working-class demands.[11]

This activism tightened the links between labor and the Democratic Party. In 1934 United Mine Workers secretary-treasurer Thomas Kennedy was elected lieutenant governor on the Democratic ticket. At the same time, the Central Labor Union formally endorsed two candidates with business backgrounds who were nonetheless known for their support of labor and FDR. George Earle, vice president of his family's Pennsylvania Sugar Company and a lifelong Republican until he switched to the Democrats in 1932, ran for governor. Joseph Guffey, president of the Guffey-Gillespie Oil Company, ran for a seat in the U.S. Senate. Both men won historic victories that ended decades of Republican power. The Democratic platform called for the abolition of sweatshops, better workman's compensation, a minimum wage, the end of private corporate police, and laws recognizing the right of unionization and collective bargaining. With several union officials sitting in the legislature while Kennedy ran the senate, labor achieved many of these goals and advanced its interests more than at any time in the state's past.[12]

Working-class political activism permeated the city and state but found its greatest expression in the Pennsylvania Labor Non-Partisan League. The league was founded in August 1936 with the purpose of supporting pro-labor candidates. Patrick Fagan of the United Mine Workers chaired the organization while the ACWA's Charles Weinstein was vice chairman. Other active unions included the ILGWU, the Brewery Workers, and the United

Textile Workers. In all, the league attracted some one hundred fifty thousand members and raised $81,000 in support of its candidates. Although nominally nonpartisan, the league backed Democratic candidates at all levels and threw its strongest support to Franklin Roosevelt. In such pamphlets as *Roosevelt and Labor* and *He Fights for Labor*, league activists reminded Pennsylvanians that the president had helped them on a range of issues, including collective bargaining, shorter hours, and economic security. Over the course of the 1936 campaign, the league distributed 7.5 million pieces of literature and used nine soundtrucks to get out the word on FDR. The league also held rallies across the state, mostly in industrial and coalmining areas, and broadcast some of them on the radio. The president spoke to 50,000 people at one of these rallies, while Governor Earle addressed a throng of 225,000 at another. By the end of the 1936 campaign, the league was holding a rally in Philadelphia every night.[13]

There was no question where Philadelphia's working class stood in the 1936 election. "The issue of 'Stand by Roosevelt' will overshadow everything else," wrote the editors of the *United Mine Workers Journal*. "Labor knows its friends, and it knows that President Roosevelt is a real friend. . . . Never before did labor so unanimously support a candidate for President." When election day arrived, ordinary Philadelphians backed up the Mine Workers' claim. The president carried Philadelphia by 210,000 votes, and in South Philadelphia, where many garment workers lived, FDR received 80 percent of the ballots. Working-class political activism, from Non-Partisan League rallies to debates in people's homes, had energized Democratic politics and helped keep Franklin Roosevelt in the White House.[14]

This was a great moment for the Democrats and organized labor, but problems lurked beneath the surface. Despite labor's solidarity in support of Roosevelt, race threatened the city's working-class unity. CIO leaders, in part because of conviction and in part because heavy industry had so many white ethnic groups and African Americans, had committed themselves to racial equality from the start. Philip Murray, the chairman of the Steel Workers Organizing Committee, made the point clear to black Philadelphians. "[The CIO holds] the firm belief," he told a meeting of the city's African Americans in 1937, "that . . . each national union should admit to membership upon a basis of absolute equality every man and woman eligible to membership, regardless of race, creed, political or religious belief." Studies showed, however, that despite the CIO's good intentions, few blacks in Philadelphia actually belonged to unions. The National Maritime Union and the United Electrical, Radio and Machine Workers took in a few African Americans, but other labor organizations openly discriminated. Philadelphia-area CIO leaders who practiced nondiscrimination themselves knew that rank-and-file white workers often balked at working with blacks. "If the employer just hires a Negro and sends him in to work with white people who have not been warned by their union, there may be trouble," one organizer said. CIO leaders meant what they said about accepting blacks, but many African Americans knew that actually getting in a union was another matter.[15]

Whatever the CIO's problems, the AFL was far worse. Nationally, AFL unions were known for their openly discriminatory practices, often writing Jim Crow regulations into their constitutions. The Brotherhood of Railroad Trainmen and the Pipe Fitters were the most obvious examples of racist AFL unions, but they were merely two of many. In Philadelphia, AFL unions, such as the bookbinders, machinists, and brewerymen, refused to admit African Americans into apprenticeship programs, and many of those who got training elsewhere could not find skilled work. This relegated as many as 90 percent of working black women and 60 percent of black men to domestic work. The rest took jobs as day laborers. According to studies conducted between 1900 and 1935 (the pre-CIO era), African Americans made up less than one percent of the city's unionized workforce, and most black union members were in all-black organizations, such as the hod carriers. Philadelphia's workplaces, in the words of the historian Walter Licht, had a "separate labor market" for blacks, and conflicts over jobs provided a constant source of irritation in working-class Philadelphia.[16]

The other significant tension within the labor movement was the split between the AFL and the CIO. Although the AFL did become more activist after the onset of the Depression, organization leaders were never comfortable working with radicals. In the early 1930s, AFL leaders avoided Communist-led marches and the CP's Trade Union Unity League. A few years later they tended to view the newly established CIO, with its confrontational tactics and leftist organizers, as far too radical as well. Even more, AFL leaders harbored a deep-seated animosity toward industrial unions stemming from the CIO's split from their organization. These tensions occasionally bubbled to the surface. In 1937, for instance, AFL organizer Lewis Hines purged the AFL of all members suspected of harboring Communist sympathies. In July of that year the AFL and CIO clashed as both attempted to organize the city's truck drivers. Over the course of several days, in the words of a federal investigator, "a driver was dragged from his truck and stabbed, cabs and trucks were overturned and set afire, and much property was damaged or destroyed." The mayor finally calmed the city by calling in extra police and declaring a state of emergency. While these tensions over race and ideology undoubtedly damaged working-class solidarity, the city's workers held together in the mid-1930s and translated their unity into support for Franklin Roosevelt and the New Deal. How long that unity would hold was another question.[17]

The Communist Party

Philadelphia's Communist Party, while much smaller than organized labor, was another source of the left-of-center politics that eventually provided institutional support for the Democratic Party. The city's CP, like the national party, reached its peak in the mid- to late 1930s, when some thirty-five hundred people joined and thousands more "fellow travelers" signed petitions, attended rallies, and marched on city hall. Beyond the formal party lay a web of affiliated organizations that connected thousands more with the CP. These groups, which seldom lasted more than a few years, dealt with foreign policy (the American League for Peace and Democracy), civil rights and civil liberties (the International Labor Defense, the Civil Rights Congress, the National Negro Congress), labor (the Trade Union Unity League and its unemployed councils), and youth (American Youth for Democracy), among other issues. Progressive Philadelphians of the 1930s may not have belonged to the Communist Party, but chances were they knew someone who did or at least someone affiliated with one of these organizations.[18]

Membership in the party represented a cross-section of working-class Philadelphia, albeit one heavily tilted toward Jews. Jews constituted about two-thirds of the membership, with Protestants making up 20 percent and Catholics 15 percent. The parents of many members were born in Eastern Europe, and they brought at least a rudimentary radical politics with them when they immigrated. African Americans also had a large presence in the party, making up about one-tenth of its membership but nearly one-half of those members whose parents were native-born. Seldom had these African Americans had a radical upbringing, but their experiences of poverty, exacerbated by the Depression and Philadelphia's racist culture, made the party's program enticing.[19]

The city's minority populations split over the Communist Party. On the one hand, the CP offered a compelling critique of American capitalism, particularly in the depths of the Depression. On the other hand, many Philadelphians were afraid that joining the party would push them even further away from America's mainstream and perhaps alienate them from their religious faith. Philadelphia's black population offers a prominent example of this division. While many African Americans disagreed with the party's

The Communist Party led a number of marches through Center City in the early 1930s. In response to the economic devastation of the Great Depression, Philadelphia's left-wing activists came to support Franklin Roosevelt by the mid-1930s and formed a vital part of the Democratic coalition. Courtesy of Temple University Libraries, Urban Archives, Philadelphia PA.

larger philosophy, they respected its egalitarian practices. The CP's defense of the Scottsboro Boys, for example, led many people to sign petitions, attend meetings, and donate money to the International Labor Defense (the party's legal arm). Religious leaders and the Young Women's Christian Association (YWCA) were impressed enough with the party that they let the CP hold meetings in their buildings. And Thomas Nabried and Ed Strong held leadership positions in the 1940s and 1950s. E. Washington Rhodes, on the other hand, worried that there could soon be "more dark-skinned than white communists in Philadelphia." This was a problem, he believed, because the Communists' "ideology was not in keeping with the ideas and traditions of American black people." But Rhodes did understand the CP's appeal. "When it is considered that equality is the theory of Communism, and that inequality is the result of the present system," Rhodes wrote, "it is amazing that millions of Negroes have not joined the followers of the Red flag." Despite reservations about the party, many blacks did join hands with their working-class counterparts in Jewish and other Euro-American communities because, as one young radical put it, "The Communists acted."[20]

In their protests over unemployment and housing, Communists helped create an atmosphere that showed political change was coming. From the earliest days of the Depression, the CP used marches on city hall to protest the government's failure to help ordinary people. The first demonstration took place in February 1930, when marchers carrying placards that read "We Want Work," "Down with Politicians," and "Organize and Fight" demonstrated at city hall. As the two hundred fifty or so protestors grew more unruly, a few decided to rush the police guards and break into the mayor's office. The guards were well prepared, and in the ensuing melee "some heads were struck," as the *Evening Bulletin* put it in a bit of understatement. The police then arrested a handful of Communists, which only strengthened their will to challenge the government. The party marched on city hall several more times over the next few weeks, using signs to urge the public to "Join the Demonstration of Unemployed" and "Demand Work or Wages." CP rhetoric captured what was wrong with Philadelphia's political system and the nation's more generally. Before the New Deal, working-class Philadelphians had no safety net, no government support when times were hard. The few private aid societies were failing, and without a job workers knew they would be out on the street. Only the government could assure their survival, and government help would come only by joining together and demanding it from city hall. Even more, the CP knew it had to press its case quickly, not only because the early Depression seemed to offer the best chance of winning converts, but also because thousands of unemployed Philadelphians were being evicted from their homes and facing starvation. Such circumstances made many people pay attention to the party's protests, and quite a few joined.[21]

By the early 1930s, conservative Philadelphians were beginning to recognize the CP as more than a passing annoyance, but as a real threat to the political order. The party kept growing in number until, in April 1932, the police broke up a demonstration of some five thousand people at city hall. On many a May Day for the rest of the decade party rallies numbered in the thousands, not the hundreds. "[There could be a] good deal of disorder in the next few months," Lorena Hickok, a reporter working for New Dealer Harry Hopkins, wrote of the city's turbulence in 1933. Businessmen worriedly agreed. "[We should] urge the jobless to shun our large cities and towns, go into the country and work raking gardens," wrote Alexander Whillidin of the Pennsylvania Railroad. "This may seem drastic, but a hungry man is dangerous." Republican leaders used police power to reassure their corporate supporters. Mayor Harry Mackey created the Red Squad to attack leftist demonstrators and had the National Guard drill to "meet the possible mob rule that might take place." Mayor Moore continued Mackey's policies. When five hundred demonstrators marched from the city dump (the only place the police had allowed them to hold their meeting) to city hall, two hundred policemen charged the crowd, driving their motorcycles into the marchers and sending seventy to the hospital. At other times, the police beat speakers in front of city hall or "belabored [them] into silence" in the *Public Ledger*'s rosier terms. Republican judges offered the Left no help, with Thomas O'Hara, for example, declaring "a war to the finish against Communism" in his courtroom. There was no need to give Communists a fair trial, he argued, because "there is all the difference in the world between Communism and Americanism." All these violations of civil liberties caused conservatives little trouble: they were happy to see their government acting forcefully. Thank you for "ridding City Hall Plaza of the hoodlum gangs," one woman wrote to Mayor Moore. The party clearly represented a threat, at least in conservatives' eyes, to Philadelphia's Republican political order.[22]

Despite the repression, the CP had enough political power to make some forays beyond street protests and into formal politics. It nominated slates of candidates at various times, including Samuel Lee, a black longshoreman, for lieutenant governor. The party platform, not surprisingly, called for reforms to help the working class: the abolition of corporate police; old-age, sickness, maternity, and unemployment pensions; and equality for African

The Communist Party posed a threat to Philadelphia's political and financial leaders, who used city police to break up CP rallies. Here a policeman attacks a party leader in 1932. Courtesy of Temple University Libraries, Urban Archives, Philadelphia PA.

Americans, among other things. But the Communists had little chance of winning elections on their own. Their real political agency came after they built the Popular Front and worked to ensure a Democratic victory in 1936.[23]

In the mid-1930s Communist organizers made their party's connections to the Democrats explicit. Adopting FDR's language, one CP leader told party members it was "absolutely necessary to defeat the economic royalists." He then vowed to withdraw all CP candidates and to raise thousands of dollars for "our New Deal election campaign." The CP was particularly interested in making sure that all laborers understood where their loyalties had to lie. "We must . . . assure victory for the New Deal in Pennsylvania and we must also involve the rank and file of the United Mine Workers, the American Federation of Labor, the fraternal and other political New Deal demonstrations to

reaching move to help black workers was its attempt to form an alliance with the CIO. Davis believed that if the NNC could establish such a relationship it could work with organized labor to build interracial alliances that would push liberal politics to the left. The campaign's Pennsylvania effort started in July 1936 when Davis asked Fauset to go to Steelton, an industrial city near Harrisburg, to organize five hundred black steelworkers, about 20 percent of the city's total. Davis thought that organizing in Steelton might lead to another NNC chapter there that would help the congress move beyond its Philadelphia boundaries. He also thought that Fauset might be able to bring these workers into the CIO's Steel Workers Organizing Committee. At the time, the steelworkers were having a hard time organizing mills across the country, and after meeting with union officials, Davis knew that they would return the favor to anyone who helped them. "If we . . . aid in bringing Negro workers into the union," Davis wrote, "we may expect large sums of money from the Steel Workers Organizing Committee to further [our efforts]." Such a campaign, Davis believed, would "bolster up the whole Congress movement among workers in basic industries" and help build an alliance between the NNC and the CIO. Ultimately he hoped that the congress would emerge with a "real trade union base." After a couple weeks of organizing, Fauset arranged for the town's three leading ministers and a number of steelworkers to establish a "permanent Congress organization," and they brought a number of workers into the union movement. After this beginning, Fauset returned to Philadelphia, letting the town's residents chart their own future.[27]

Labor and NNC leaders strengthened their alliance after Steelton. The Philadelphia NNC worked with the Pennsylvania Labor Non-Partisan League and the city's Labor Committee, for example, to build public support for Roosevelt's attempted restructuring of the U.S. Supreme Court in 1937, and Davis saw a bright future ahead. "This is simply the beginning," he told Fauset. "[We will cooperate] on many other issues such as the Anti-Lynching Bill, Civil Rights Legislation and other matters of great interest to the Negro people." In forming this alliance with organized labor, NNC leaders revealed their hope that black and labor organizations could come together to reinforce each others' political power. But, Davis knew, in order to generate that political power he had to get more ordinary African Americans involved at all levels. "I am anxious," he wrote, "that throughout the nation we indicate our ability to effectively rally the Negro people to progressive causes."[28]

Fauset knew how to "rally the Negro people": pay attention to local issues and get people involved at the grassroots level. It was critical, Fauset believed, to move away from hierarchical models and to have "an organization scheme of the widest democratic scope" so that people could have a say in their own fate. They would not long support an organization that dictated from the top down. That is why he conducted campaigns at theaters and stores in North and West Philadelphia, places that discriminated against black Philadelphians, who, he could be sure, would turn out to protest. When he followed a related strategy of circulating a petition to protest local discriminatory judges, some twenty-five thousand people signed. "The eyes of the [state] legislators nearly popped out," Fauset wrote, "when they saw all this evidence of Congress activity, and of the resentment of the masses." Fauset took his philosophy to the city's political leaders, telling Jack Kelly to "listen more attentively to the real folks down in the streets, in the lodges and in the barber shops." Fauset's grassroots approach proved wildly successful. He brought roughly one hundred fifty organizations into the Philadelphia NNC with a total membership of fifty thousand people. "I think it can safely be said by now," Fauset wrote to Davis in July 1936, that "the people of this city look more to the NNC than to any other set-up whenever questions of inter-racial relations arise."[29]

The supreme achievement for the Philadelphia NNC, and for local black activism in general in the years before World War II, was hosting the congress's national conference in 1937. The national NNC had started strongly in 1935–36, building chapters in a number of the nation's cities, but Philadelphia had perhaps the strongest of all the branches. "More constructive activity for the Negro masses," one reporter noted, "occurred in Philadelphia than in any other part of the country." Davis and Fauset wanted to use the branch's strength to stage a convention that would cement the NNC's growing reputation as a civil rights leader. "You can count on Philly . . . for the coming Congress," wrote Fauset. "Not only is our reputation at stake, but the future of the Congress movement can be made immeasurably surer by a good showing." An overjoyed Davis later told Fauset that he expected hundreds of delegates from the CIO, the Urban League, and the NAACP. He anticipated, he wrote, "a most significant meeting in Philadelphia," which would "pack Convention Hall." Neither man was disappointed.[30]

The convention energized black Philadelphia in ways seldom seen in the city's past, as for a few nights in October it became the center of political activism in the nation. Over twelve hundred delegates, representing the gamut of black organizations, from unions to religious groups to business associations, flooded the city. They came from twenty-seven states and the District of Columbia and represented the most politically active citizens of the day. Local and national speakers, from Mayor Wilson and Lieutenant

Governor Thomas Kennedy to A. Philip Randolph and Philip Murray of the Steel Workers Organizing Committee, lent an even greater air of importance to the gathering. Leaders such as these, men who wielded power in both political and labor institutions, could play a critical role in the future of African Americans, and Fauset hoped to bolster ties with them. It seemed a most auspicious moment. As one commentator observed, with tens of thousands of Philadelphians attending the evening sessions, "the Conference [took on] the air of a festival and for three days and nights . . . there was a 'power' that seemed to envelop the city."[31]

Speakers took note of the ferment they saw around them and addressed African Americans' demands. Fauset was the star of the show, delivering a ringing opening address that made black economic and civil rights demands clear. "Bad housing SHALL GO," he thundered from the podium. "Unemployment SHALL CEASE. Education of our youth SHALL BE FREE and UNLIMITED. Barriers between whites and blacks shall vanish. The Constitution of the United States shall be a vital instrument in the lives of all people, Negro and white alike." Then, speaking directly to Philadelphians in the audience, he told them that they were ready to "leap at the opportunity to move in the van of greater things for the Negro." "It is clear," he said, "that we in Philadelphia are coming to understand the meaning of unity, the power of united action."[32]

Other speakers lauded African Americans for their activism and acknowledged their right to equality in politics and the workplace. Mayor Wilson drew on the city's history to point out African Americans' just claims. The Liberty Bell, Independence Hall, and the Declaration of Independence, he argued, were part of African Americans' heritage. "They belong to all of us," he said, "they are yours and they are ours and may they forever serve as symbols of an enduring faith and unity of patriotic thought, binding together all the American people." Labor leaders focused on black rights on the job and the need for interracial unions. "In reconstructing the social order, which is part of the great work of the Negro Congress," said Thomas Kennedy, the United Mine Workers official and Democratic lieutenant governor, "we must give attention to injustice in the distribution of national wealth and income. . . . It is vitally necessary for laborers to be united in labor organizations and to be free to fight for basic and uniform [rights]." Demanding an end to discrimination on the job did not mean that African Americans wanted special privileges, Kennedy continued; rather, "They are only attempting to secure equal rights and equal opportunities and if given those equal opportunities they will work out their own destiny." Philip Murray drew the black-labor connections even tighter, telling the conference, "There is no other labor organization in this country that affords the Negro worker the same opportunity as does . . . the CIO." "We tell you," he continued, "our economic and political salvation lies in [you using] your organizations, societies, [and] churches . . . to assist the CIO in the furtherance of its campaign."[33]

The conference highlighted the growing importance of extra–New Deal black activism in Philadelphia. Labor leaders knew they needed black support to succeed and appealed to the audience to give the CIO a chance. At one point, Murray called the CIO's agenda a "crusade" that could only accomplish its goals if African Americans joined. Politicians too showed their recognition of rising black power by attending the conference and declaring that blacks, as loyal Americans, deserved equal treatment. Labor leaders and politicians, people with formal power, were listening to and seeking out Philadelphia's African Americans in ways they had not done before. In large measure, this was due to Fauset and the NNC. But the local congress only had power because of the widespread support of ordinary Philadelphians. By paying attention to the concerns of ordinary people, Fauset had built a huge, activist organization that staged one of the largest political gatherings in city history. Black Philadelphians on the left in the late 1930s were beginning to muster real political strength and to articulate a program of economic and civil rights, and that, in the end, was the historical importance of the National Negro Congress.[34]

After this crowning conference, the NNC's downfall came swiftly. Some members believed the congress depended too heavily on the CIO and the Communist Party. Others saw too many white faces in what was supposed to be a "Negro" congress. Whatever the cause of the problems, when Fauset left the organization in 1939 to devote more time to his career in education and writing, no one else could hold the branch together. The Philadelphia branch's declension mirrored that of the national organization. As Davis pulled the NNC closer to the CIO and the Communist Party, the congress dropped racial goals in favor of supporting the Soviet Union. "The National Negro Congress [above all must embody] the broad expression of anti-war and anti-imperialist struggle," said one congress official after Stalin signed the Nazi-Soviet Pact. Randolph fought the move but lost. "The Communist party," he warned, "was not primarily, or fundamentally, concerned about the Negro." Too close of an alliance with any organization was dangerous, he continued, for if the black man were to "save himself, he must depend on his own right arm!" But as Randolph looked out over the audience at the 1940 convention, he noted that white delegates sat in one-third of the seats and felt he no longer spoke to the group he had helped to create. He soon resigned, saying that the large number of whites "made the Congress look like a joke." The NNC continued to function until 1948 but lost its influence after Randolph stepped down. The congress's demise meant that a more leftist politics that had invigorated black Philadelphia by bringing together economic and civil rights issues and by forcefully pushing them to the fore lost its momentum as a more mainstream liberalism, led by those willing to work with federal agencies within the framework of the New Deal state, became the champion of racial advance. Over the next two decades, the latter approach, with its ties to federal authority and the Democratic Party, brought decidedly mixed results.[35]

The Right

As black Philadelphians expressed a more activist politics and grew closer to the Democratic Party, some members of the city's ethnic communities turned to the right. In some ways this was a direct reaction against black demands, but it also was a way to back right-wing politics in Italy and Germany. To be sure, many working-class whites abhorred the politics of the right and either ignored it or struggled against it by joining antifascist organizations. But enough white Philadelphians backed right-wing domestic and international politics that their support deepened racial fissures within the city's working class, and this weakened the Democratic Party just as African Americans were moving more solidly toward it. At the same time, Republican politicians in the late 1930s began using race more earnestly as a tool to widen divisions between ordinary Philadelphians and thus undermine progressive politics. Several trends—a more assertive black politics that drew African Americans closer to the Democratic Party, the rightward drift of some members of Philadelphia's ethnic communities, and the GOP's growing use of racial politics—worked together to undercut racial solidarity and damage liberalism in Philadelphia.

Fascism started out as a source of pride in Philadelphia's Italian community. Italian Philadelphians organized their first fascist organization in 1921, a year before Benito Mussolini took power, and until the United States went to war with Italy two decades later, they offered overwhelming support to their homeland's government. Local newspapers exalted every fascist victory while local leaders, such as Giovanni Di Silvestro, announced that he and his fellow countrymen were "heart and soul" with Mussolini. For profascists in the early 1930s, the ideology did not embody the evil overtones it later assumed. Instead, it promised to create a modern, efficient state with a strong military and a growing empire that would enable Italy to assume its "rightful" place among the world powers. This vision of their homeland's destiny is what led most Italian Americans to look with pride on Italy's fascist government. They believed that Italy would no longer be a poor, politically divided, agrarian country; instead, it would now become an equal among the world's industrial nations. After Mussolini took control, one man recalled, "No one called us wops."[36]

Italy's invasion of Ethiopia in 1935 demonstrated the racism inherent in fascism and caused bitter feelings between blacks and Italians. In articles and political cartoons Philadelphia's black press portrayed the invasion as a white bully attacking a small black child, and African Americans were indignant that Italian Americans could support such a thing. The *Tribune* put the matter pointedly when it argued that the invasion was about more than a grab for oil and minerals. "Ethiopians are told that they are a backward people," the editors wrote. "They have no right to keep their rich oil lands and fertile fields from the grasping hands of civilization. . . . The same gospel preached by the Chief Justice Taney of the U.S. Supreme Court when he said 'Colored people have no rights which white people are bound to respect' is the idea back of the attack on Ethiopia." Italian American leaders enraged African Americans by arguing that those opposed to Italy's invasion were "too uneducated to realize that Mussolini planned to civilize that country" and that any Ethiopian defense was simply "proof of the barbarism of black people." Tensions reached the point where blacks staged boycotts of some Italian merchants; a riot almost broke out after a man drove his truck through Italian South Philadelphia with signs urging African Americans to continue their actions; and the city canceled a Friends of Italy victory parade designed to celebrate Ethiopia's capitulation for fear of interracial violence. African Americans held onto the issue long after the invasion ended, with NNC panels discussing how to fight for Ethiopia's independence and the *Tribune* running such headlines as "Ethiopian Women Raped Wholesale by Italians; Abdomens Bayoneted." Black-Italian relations never really recovered from these strains.[37]

Much like the issue of Ethiopia, the rise of the controversial cleric Father Charles Coughlin also showed the limits of interracialism within the city. Coughlin, a Roman Catholic priest based in the Detroit area, used his weekly radio addresses to become the most famous clergyman in America, attracting as many as forty-five million listeners in the early 1930s. At first Coughlin supported FDR, telling his audience, "The New Deal is Christ's deal." But over the next few years he came to identify the federal government with

Jewish interests and by 1936 had broken with the president and become virulently anti-Semitic. By 1938, writes the historian Alan Brinkley, Coughlin was "an outspoken anti-Semite, a rabid anti-communist, a strident isolationist, and, increasingly, a cautious admirer of Benito Mussolini and Adolf Hitler." He had a huge following in Philadelphia.[38]

Coughlin's loyalists in Philadelphia, mostly men and women of Irish descent, attacked Jews and blacks, both of whom they regarded as their enemies. His organization, the Christian Front, never enjoyed a large formal membership (one estimate put the number at about four hundred), but Coughlin had a massive grassroots following. In a radio station's poll to see whether it should run concert music or Coughlin's broadcasts, the vote came in at 187,000 for Coughlin, 12,000 for the music. These people put Coughlin's sermons, their beliefs, into action. They plastered anti-Semitic stickers on synagogues and Jewish-owned stores, smashed synagogue windows, and disrupted Jewish meetings in West Philadelphia. They also threw rocks through the windows of black churches, broke up black-Jewish meetings of the Committee for Racial and Religious Tolerance, and started a riot in West Philadelphia to terrify blacks in that neighborhood. Coughlin's largest groups of supporters lived in heavily Irish Kensington and West Philadelphia, where residents violently resisted African Americans and Jews moving into their neighborhoods. Several commentators in fact called Irish West Philadelphia "one of the most virulent centers of anti-Semitic and antidemocratic agitation in the entire country." Things finally got so bad that residents there established the West Philadelphia Interracial Forum to try to soothe tensions.[39]

The Bund put further strains on race relations in Philadelphia. German Americans made up the bulk of this pro-Nazi organization, but there were many Irish members as well. Estimates put formal membership at around four hundred, but thousands turned out for meetings and kept informed of Bund activities. Leaders repeatedly told audiences that they must solve the "racial question." There could be no "interracial" culture, they believed, because of "the profound, ineradicable racial differences between the Aryan, in other words, White Gentile races on the one hand, and the Asiatic, African and other non-Aryan races on the other." They also despised the Roosevelt administration. One man told an audience that the Bund wanted to "rid America of President Rosenfeld, his New Deal and the nation's Jewish democracy . . . by learning a few lessons from the smart nations abroad." Related groups, such as the League for Protestant Action, used similar rhetoric, arguing that its members had to support candidates who would oppose those "racial and sectarian groups . . . ascendant in our political life today." Their candidates of choice came from the GOP.[40]

Republicans saw this rightward drift and tried to harness it for their own purposes. Their first strategy was to charge the New Deal with being "un-American" and "Communistic." Gubernatorial candidate Arthur James charged that the New Deal "undermined our government," the WPA pushed "economic slavery," and state regulation of business was "a curse [because] it destroyed initiative and ambition." The *Inquirer* connected Governor Earle to CIO head John L. Lewis, emphatically urging Philadelphians to "VOTE AGAINST LEWIS AND THE COMMUNISTS! VOTE FOR STRAIGHT AMERICANISM, BY VOTING FOR ARTHUR JAMES FOR GOVERNOR!" And Republican Senate candidate Jay Cooke told crowds that administration officials were "either outright Reds, or as pink as a broiled lobster."[41]

A number of Republicans went beyond this rhetoric and supported groups like the Bund, which had made its racial politics clear. At the Bund's German Day meeting in 1939, Senator James Davis gave a speech and Congressmen James McGranery and Fred Gartner sat in the audience. The Bund kept their Nazi paraphernalia mostly out of sight, but the audience responded to Davis's speech with "Heils" and Adolf Hitler salutes. Bund leaders appreciated the GOP's support and its political views, telling members to vote Republican to help "destroy Communism and bring to a success the hope for government by and for Aryans." They also assured their members that if Arthur James, the Republican gubernatorial candidate, should win in 1938, then "our organization will bear the friendship . . . [of] the Republican Party."[42]

Not just Bund members appreciated the Republicans' views. So-called native whites, mostly Protestants of northern and western European descent who lived chiefly in the new neighborhoods on the edges of the city and in the bordering counties, strongly supported the Republicans, giving the GOP some 70 percent of their ballots in the late 1930s. These people had never swung completely to Roosevelt so were not a huge Democratic loss, but their overwhelming support for the GOP worried Democrats, who feared that similar tallies in the 1940 election could end the New Deal. These native whites were not just deserting or refusing to join the Democrats, they were voting for Republican candidates who knew the racialized propaganda of the Bund and its right-wing allies and chose to associate with them anyway. Fred Gartner, who won his race for the U.S. House of Representatives from northeast Philadelphia, was the most prominent example of these Bund-allied candidates. But others showed similar views, with Governor James vowing to dismantle the new Civil Rights Bureau upon taking office. The racial divide in Philadelphia politics was becoming clearer.[43]

The 1940 Election

Democrats worried that these racial issues would defeat Roosevelt in 1940, but more than race troubled liberals in the late 1930s. The president's missteps—his failed court-packing plan, the 1937 recession, and so on—helped the Republicans pick up eighty-one seats in the U.S. House and eight in the Senate as well as thirteen governorships in 1938. In Pennsylvania, local issues added to the Democrats' problems. Jack Kelly, David Lawrence (Pittsburgh's Democratic leader), Governor Earle, and Senator Guffey squabbled endlessly over the distribution of patronage and the choice of nominees for office. As each faction within the Democratic Party maneuvered for power, it charged the others with corruption and venality. While party leaders sniped at each other, the city's poorest voters grew disgruntled with the Democrats. The president's party seemed more worried about intramural politics than keeping the WPA and public housing alive. Remnants of the Republican machine looked better and better to these people: at least ward leaders lived nearby and could provide food, clothing, and a little money when times got bad. One poor African American told an investigator that he knew many blacks who were angry "over being laid off" from government jobs and "having to wait [to] go on relief." It would not be hard, he implied, for them to desert the Democratic Party. And in 1938, for a variety of reasons, ranging from racism to disenchantment with the New Deal, many voters did just that. Governor Earle, who had won a smashing victory in 1934, lost by nearly 400,000 votes in his race for the Senate while Charles Jones, who sought to succeed Earle in the governor's mansion, lost by 208,000 votes. Overall, the Italian and Irish Democratic votes dropped by 13 and 7 percent, respectively. Combined with the results from the native white communities, the Democrats were tottering.[44]

Despite all these problems, the city went for Roosevelt in 1940. In part, Philadelphians voted for FDR because the election took place in the context of a European war that threatened American security. "We believe," said the members of a local "Draft Roosevelt" movement, that "for the safety of the nation itself . . . it is indispensable that the one who led the nation out of bondage should continue to be its leader." Americans in general trusted Roosevelt—60 percent to Wendell Willkie's 40 percent, according to one Gallup poll—to lead the country through the difficult times that obviously lay ahead. But efforts by Kelly and other local party leaders played a role as well. They urged Roosevelt to make two or three visits to the city in order to solidify his support. Kelly also stumped for FDR in the city's working-class communities and helped get a crowd of one hundred thousand to turn out for a Roosevelt speech at Convention Hall. African Americans and Jews, both targets of far-right organizations that were building bridges to the Republican Party, provided the Democrats with their strongest support: Jews with over 80 percent of their vote and African Americans with 63 percent. Their belief in the New Deal and skepticism that the Republicans would offer anything better kept them in the party. The Irish and Italian votes were a little lower, at 58 and 60 percent, respectively, with the Italian vote falling nearly ten points since the 1936 election. Despite all of the tensions, Philadelphians had come together for FDR in 1940, and overjoyed Democrats once again crowded into downtown streets to celebrate their victory. Although one conservative sniffed that the revelry "sounded like the noises of uncouth hoodlums to me," November 5 was the Democrats' day.[45]

The 1940 election brought Philadelphia's New Deal–era politics to a close. Over the previous eight years the Democrats had tried to craft a liberal coalition. Labor and the Left, Euro- and African American community leaders, and Irish and Jewish businessmen had all worked together to try to build an alliance. At times it worked, particularly when Roosevelt was on the ballot and the New Deal was plainly making people's lives better. But manifold tensions always lurked just below the surface. By the end of the 1930s these tensions had grown more obvious, particularly as a more prominent and insistent black political activism fueled a rising white reaction that found expression in the support of right-wing racist groups with budding ties to the GOP. Black political activism continued to grow in the following decades, tightening the links between African Americans and the Democratic Party. During the World War II years, as tens of thousands of African Americans moved to Philadelphia and the city's housing and job markets came under great strain, tensions increased between Irish, Italian, and black Philadelphians. Key Republican leaders, recognizing these race-based divisions, deliberately linked African American advancement to the Democratic Party and thereby purposely fanned the flames that brought the city's tenuous liberal interracial alliance crashing to the ground.

World War II

Semitic attacks," as the Fellowship Commission put it, so disturbed many Philadelphians that the city created the Fair Election Campaign Code and enacted a city ordinance outlawing anonymous hate propaganda.[41]

Although the election led to reforms to control racial and ethnic slurs, the Republicans had found a winning strategy for attacking Democratic politicians and constructing an effective politics of their own. Their strategy depended in part on pointing to the Roosevelt administration and candidates friendly to it as outsiders promoting social programs that raised taxes and drained the pockets of white working people. But it also depended on explicit attacks on some of the Democratic Party's key supporters. For the most part, Republicans were not yet entirely ready to write off the black vote: they did accuse Bullitt of being a racist after all, in hopes that some African Americans would continue to vote for the party of Lincoln. But at the same time, Samuel refused to speak to black groups or even to address their issues, and he was widely regarded as an enemy of public housing and other interests important to the black community. Still, his smears against Bullitt and the continuing hold of the Republican machine in the river wards brought many African Americans into Samuel's camp. He won 54 percent of their vote, although blacks did vote more heavily Democratic than did any other group except for Jews. With the black vote obviously still in play, Republicans in later years would have to ask themselves if pursuing it was worth possibly losing the support of Euro-Americans. Most would answer no.

The sharpest split was between Philadelphia's Italian and Jewish communities. Jewish voters were well aware of Samuel's blatantly anti-Semitic pamphlet and gave Bullitt 59 percent of their vote. This total was well below the 81 percent they gave to Roosevelt in 1940, but that was more an indication that many Democratic voters, whatever their ethnicity, were Roosevelt supporters more than anything else. Italian Americans, on the other hand, cast only 34 percent of their votes for Bullitt. In part, their vote was a measure of their discontent with FDR, who had accepted the Alien Registration Act, which stigmatized Italian immigrants as possible traitors. That the United States, under a Democratic president and Congress, had just finished waging war against Italy did not help Bullitt either. But Samuel's views on blacks certainly did him no harm in Italian South Philadelphia, where Hugo Maiale, the foremost contemporary observer of the community, noted, "To arouse the prejudice of Italians against Negroes is always a good line of attack when no other succeeds." Philadelphia's politics had too many different peoples involved merely to mimic the black-white racial demagoguery of the South, but the 1943 election showed that race was becoming a central issue in the city's politics and that Republicans were instrumental in fostering and then exploiting racial tensions.[42]

These first years of World War II presaged events to come in Philadelphia. The African American battle for adequate housing and equal access to jobs grew more intense in the coming years. The context of war and black involvement with the Democratic Party, though shaky in Bullitt's campaign, gave African Americans the platform to expand their liberal political activism and demand an end to discrimination. To maintain this platform they increasingly allied themselves with the government, particularly Democratic officials. As this alliance grew, some groups, primarily Jews, supported black rights and stayed with the Democratic Party. Others, such as Italian and Irish Americans, questioned what they could gain from a party building an alliance with African Americans. If blacks won better jobs and housing through the FEPC and the U.S. Housing Administration, what resources, white workers wondered, would be left to help them? Surely, they thought, promoting black rights would do them little good, and certainly that was not the reason they had supported Roosevelt and his New Deal in the first place. These issues would come to a head in the battle for jobs at the Philadelphia Transportation Company, where rising black activism clashed with burgeoning white resentment, and the results were explosive.

Black Activism and the PTC

When your boys come back and you meet them in Broad Street
Station and look into their eyes—no, they may not have eyes!
When you shake their hand—no, they may have left part of their
bodies on some God-forsaken beach! When they ask you, "Are we
driving trolleys yet?" if you cannot tell them "yes"...
—Adam Clayton Powell Jr. at a PTC rally, 1943

A vote for the "CIO" is a vote for Niggers on the job.
—AFL speaker, 1944

Some of the black protestors marching toward city hall in November 1943 carried American flags. Others bore placards that read "In Democracy, Freedom to Work Belongs to All," "PTC Sabotages the War Effort. Negroes Want to Work!" and "We Drive Tanks, Why Not Trolleys?" In the midst of a war for democracy, black Philadelphians had decided they could no longer accept discrimination at the Philadelphia Transportation Company (PTC). For the tens of thousands of African Americans who rode PTC vehicles every day and saw nothing but white drivers, Jim Crow at the transit company was a blatant reminder of their second-class status. Throughout the march, protestors stopped to listen to speakers argue that their efforts to end segregation at home were part of the larger war going on around them. "We are trying," said Reverend E. Luther Cunningham, "to preserve democracy on the home front as our boys are doing on the firing line." "Colored citizens pay taxes, buy war bonds, are giving their all in this war," added William Johnson of Mother Bethel African Methodist Episcopal Church. "They should not and will not be discriminated against."[1]

Over the next two months, white PTC employees reacted to this activism. Black promotions, one man told the FEPC just months after the Detroit riots, would lead to "chaos and impairment to the transportation of workers to and from the war industries." He refused to elaborate, but the committee knew just what he meant by "chaos." Others told congressional inquisitors that "the colored employee is not acceptable" and warned that they might strike rather than agree to African Americans taking "white" driving jobs at the PTC. These threats came to fruition on August 1, 1944, when white workers at the PTC walked off the job, bringing the city to a halt. Events leading to that strike revealed how many white workers were coming to see the Roosevelt administration, particularly as represented by the FEPC, as beholden to blacks and consequently as a threat to white prerogatives. Perhaps, these white workers thought, they had more to gain by allying themselves with corporate management and reactionary politicians than by siding with African Americans, the federal government, and the more egalitarian CIO.[2]

The Philadelphia Transportation Company

The push to end segregation in the PTC came from rank-and-file black workers in the company. African Americans had worked for the PTC for decades, and for a time many regarded it as a stable, friendly employer. As late as 1939 it was, one newspaperman wrote, one of the "greatest employers of Negroes in the city." Some observers worried that the company limited black jobs to maintenance, janitorial, and porter work, but during the Depression most people were just happy that the PTC kept blacks employed. The war era, with its rhetoric of democracy and a tighter labor market, brought this acquiescence to an end. In August 1941, Roosevelt Neal, Raleigh Johnson, and other longtime PTC employees formed the Committee for Equal Job Opportunity of PTC Employees and asked PTC president Ralph Senter to end discrimination at the company. In their appeal they espoused a politics of democracy and fairness that drew on the moral authority of President Roosevelt. "May we remind you," they wrote, "that not long ago, Hon. Franklin Delano Roosevelt . . . declared [discrimination to be] against 'Democratic Principles,' and promised he would do all in his power to see that all American Citizens had a fair opportunity." The employees then asked Senter to meet with them, which he did. But after listening to their arguments he refused to make any commitment. The problem, he explained, had to do with the so-called customs clause in the company's contract with its union, which forbade changing the agreement unless both parties accepted a revision. He then told the committee members that they would have to take their proposition up with their union and dismissed them from his office.[3]

Senter's position placed the onus squarely on the Philadelphia Rapid Transit Employees Union (PRTEU), which he knew would never agree to black promotions. PTC management had dominated its employees' representatives for over thirty years thanks to a disastrous 1910 trolley strike that destroyed the old union, the Keystone Carmen, and brought the well-known savior of transit companies, Thomas Mitten, to town. Mitten introduced the Cooperative Plan, which gave employees a few shares of stock in the company in exchange for lower wages and corporate control of the cooperative's leadership. Managerial control of the PTC workers' representatives—in effect a company union—lasted until 1937, when Pennsylvania passed a law modeled on the Wagner Act, which, among other things, outlawed company unions. PTC officials, led by Dr. A. A. Mitten, the deceased Thomas Mitten's son, then met with their loyalists in the workforce to establish a new union, the PRTEU. From the start of this new union, management, abetted by a group of faithful employees, used several strategies to maintain control of their workers. The PTC loaned the union's founders $7,000 to start their organization and paid the union leaders' salaries of $6,000 per year. Management also allowed PRTEU organizers to threaten employees with the loss of their jobs if they refused to join and agreed to a check-off system that let the union automatically deduct dues from employees' paychecks. To outside labor leaders, this last concession was the most suspicious: companies usually fought the provision because it helped to solidify a union's presence by guaranteeing a stream of income. Despite what looked to be obvious evidence of collusion, PRTEU leaders maintained that they operated free of company control, and the government let the union stand.[4]

With the PRTEU in place, management had a pliant "foe," more like a partner, at the bargaining table. Every contract was a bad one for the workers. They had some of the lowest wages in the industry, running 5 to 10 percent behind other big cities, such as Chicago, Detroit, and New York. They had the worst working conditions too, with drivers receiving no pay for overtime or holiday work and having to work swing runs that required them to be on the job for fourteen hours straight even though they only got paid for the eight they were on the road. Certainly many workers grumbled about how little the PTC and PRTEU offered, but they stayed with the company for decades nonetheless. In part, they did so because they saw working at the transit company as an honorable career. But PTC employment stood for more than that: to many workers it represented an inheritance they could pass down to their children. They might not be able to put their kids through college, or even aspire to such a goal, but transit workers knew they could always get work for their kids. In the mid- to late 1940s, over one-half of all PTC employees had worked for the company for at least fifteen years, and more than a quarter claimed twenty-five years of service. The company's turnover rate was a scant 1 percent, one-third of the city average and less than one quarter of the national mark.[5]

These workers counted on their jobs, counted on passing them down to their kids, and having just come through the Depression, they wanted every driving job reserved for themselves. That sentiment gave the PRTEU its power.

Union leaders might not bring better wages or working conditions, but they could guarantee to preserve PTC jobs from outside threats, and "threats" meant African Americans. The workforce of nearly ten thousand, mostly men of Irish and Italian descent, knew blacks had demanded employment at the Pennsylvania Railroad, Sun Ship, and many other companies. The PTC could not be far behind, and the PRTEU stood as a bulwark against this advancement. In part, the PRTEU protected the drivers' "psychological wage" that ensured their sole access to the company's better jobs, gave them greater security in those years just after the Depression, and granted a measure of superiority over the city's African Americans. But while the wage was "psychological" in some ways, it also brought real benefits. The PRTEU, with the company's consent, limited African Americans to dirty and menial labor while reserving the safest, best-paying jobs for whites. Blacks could join the union and work as mechanics and messengers, porters and track layers, but as the NAACP's *Crisis* observed, "regardless of training capacity, years of service, loyalty or desire a Negro could never hope to fill certain jobs, such as conductors, motormen, [or] bus drivers." The liberal newspaper *PM* added, "PTC has operated along Southern lines [for years, and white workers have] simply accepted the fact that [driving] is a white man's job, and no Negro is going to get it." More bluntly, one union official reportedly told several drivers he would "see to it that no damned n——rs ever got to drive trolley cars in Philadelphia."[6]

Raleigh Johnson and the other members of his committee knew this PTC history as well as anyone. So when Senter told them to take up their proposition with the union, Johnson expected to get rejected. He was right. The PRTEU's president, Frank Carney, refused to meet with Johnson for several months before finally saying he "would not consider [black promotions] unless told to do so by the [union's] delegates." This, Johnson knew, would never happen, and he turned to the NAACP for help.[7]

The NAACP

Until the World War II era, a worker like Johnson would likely have dismissed out of hand the thought of asking the NAACP for support. The generally held view among black Philadelphians was that the association had little interest in the problems of working people. The city's black elite ran the local association and, like their peers in most northern cities, sought "respectability" through their work with the organization, which brought higher status for them in the black community and acceptance in white society. Throughout the 1920s and 1930s, they sponsored violin concerts and poetry readings, protested exclusionary practices on tour boats on the Delaware River, and arranged "Reconciliation Trips" that brought white middle-class citizens to South Philadelphia, where they could take tours of the NAACP headquarters and meet "respectable" African Americans. These activities and events, elites felt, would uplift the masses by breaking the common man's bad habits and introducing a little "culture" into the community. Working-class issues per se never appeared on the agenda, but branch leaders believed that by ingratiating themselves to the white power structure and reforming the working-class members of their race they would help all of the city's African Americans. Not everyone accepted the NAACP's rationale. "If the officers of our local branch have accomplished anything . . . we would like to know it," wrote one columnist. "If they righted one wrong in this community, made a concerted honest-to-goodness fight on Segregation in any of its hideous forms . . . we'd like to be shown." Working-class blacks agreed, finding the organization largely irrelevant until Carolyn Davenport Moore arrived in September 1942 and began to change the culture of the association so that it helped ordinary Philadelphians.[8]

In her tenure in Philadelphia, Moore jettisoned the violin concerts and poetry readings in favor of taking up causes that working-class black Philadelphians found vital. In particular, she attacked housing and employment discrimination and did so in such an effective way that ordinary African Americans flocked to the NAACP: the branch gained eleven thousand new members during her three-year tenure. The fact that Johnson and his committee were fighting workplace discrimination, then, fit Moore's agenda perfectly. She marshaled the NAACP's resources and energized black Philadelphia in a campaign to break Jim Crow in a vital industry. Throughout the battle for driving jobs, Moore primarily relied on protest meetings and marches that encouraged ordinary Philadelphians to get involved. African Americans conducted marches from black churches and the YWCA to city hall, they distributed signs and placards that challenged the company's egregious policies, they drafted and signed petitions, and they filed grievances with the FEPC. This grassroots activism demonstrated the power of black protest in the city and highlighted the demands that African Americans were willing to make on American society as a whole.[9]

It was no accident that the PTC became the arena for that protest. The city's buses and trolleys, unavoidable conveyances given wartime gas rationing, served as focal points of persistent interracial friction. Blacks and whites might live in different neighborhoods, eat in different restaurants, and go to different churches, but when they got on a bus, they got on together. It was

When the local NAACP adopted a more grassroots approach in the early 1940s, it became a critical support center for black Philadelphians. Two of the organization's most important leaders are pictured in the front row: President Theodore Spaulding and, to his left, Executive Secretary Carolyn Davenport Moore. Courtesy of Temple University Libraries, Urban Archives, Philadelphia PA. Used by permission of the National Association for the Advancement of Colored People.

Carolyn Davenport Moore conducts a membership drive for the NAACP during World War II. The chapter's activism, often with Moore in the lead, sparked eleven thousand Philadelphians to join the local civil rights organization. Courtesy of Temple University Libraries, Urban Archives, Philadelphia PA. Used by permission of the National Association for the Advancement of Colored People.

not, however, an egalitarian experience. White passengers refused to sit next to blacks, and African Americans took umbrage at what that refusal implied. Helena O'Donnell, a Center City resident, typified the white view and expressed some of the anxiety that Irish Philadelphians felt about their own racial status: sitting next to blacks, she implied, might make her less white. "They get into the cars," she wrote, "jostle the white people, sometimes rubbing the white off our arms in summer if possible, sit all over us and in general act extremely rude. . . . [The government should] reserve a section in the car . . . and keep us separated." Drivers often made matters worse, closing the doors before black passengers could get on board and sometimes speeding past stops to leave people stranded. Some African Americans retaliated by dropping their fares on the floor or even spitting in drivers' faces. One woman became so enraged that she beat a driver badly enough to put him in the hospital. Full-fledged race riots nearly exploded on at least two occasions, once when several marines got in a brawl with a streetcar full of black workers and another time when a number of drivers dragged a teenager into their carbarn in West Philadelphia and beat him nearly to death.[10]

That the PTC was a semipublic company made the problems all the more galling but also offered a route of attack. Since the turn of the century the city had maintained a complex relationship with the transit system that in effect made the municipal government a partner with the company's financial backers. The city and private stockholders shared the company's profits, and the mayor and four other citizens sat on the PTC's board of directors. African Americans had to hand over one hundred thousand dollars a week in fares and to pay taxes to support a public entity that refused to hire them or treat them like other citizens. This was, the *Pittsburgh Courier* asserted, "tantamount to discrimination by the City of Philadelphia," and few things infuriated African Americans more. But people also knew that the company's public nature made it vulnerable to mass protest. "Negroes pay taxes," one NAACP flier read, "and their money helps to sustain the system! We demand fair employment practices by all public utilities, especially PTC." If blacks could crack this utility, the one most open to public influence, other utilities would follow, they believed. "Negro citizens," noted one reporter, "feel that if the PTC could be 'broken' the Philadelphia Electric, Bell Telephone and Philadelphia Gas Works would follow in opening the employment door to Negroes." The PTC campaign, then, was important for the jobs it could open in transit work, but its implications reached much further. Arthur Huff Fauset put the case most forcefully. "We have only begun to fight," he wrote. "PTC is a prelude to battle against all forms of discrimination not only in Philadelphia but throughout our country. It is more than a prelude to battle against discrimination, it is war against Fascism!"[11]

This community attitude toward the PTC meant that Moore helped organize a population increasingly prepared to make demands on the state and predisposed to seeing the importance of the PTC fight. To focus PTC activism, Moore framed her appeals around the rhetoric of citizenship and the need for mass involvement. She had the NAACP distribute fliers asking African Americans if they wanted to be first-class citizens and if so, telling them to write letters of protest to the PTC. She circulated descriptions of NAACP activities in the PTC campaign to churches, unions, and civic groups and urged them to get involved. And she issued "Action Notes" that told people about the NAACP's weekly meetings and offered a list of things they could do to pressure the company: draft petitions, apply for PTC jobs, go to the FEPC when their application got rejected, help on picket lines, and contact the mayor. "We are in the front lines in the battle for democracy just as much as if we were in the fox holes of the Solomons," she told her readers. "Every person who wants real democracy must get into the struggle."[12]

Just months after meeting with Johnson's committee, Moore was able to focus her community enough to put together two protest rallies. These "indignation meetings," as Moore called them, used the rhetoric of democracy to challenge Philadelphia to live up to the nation's wartime ideals. The first meeting, in March 1943, brought over a thousand people to O. V. Catto Auditorium, where the audience listened to a number of rousing speeches and then pledged in a mass resolution to "express by letters, telegrams and public announcement its condemnation of the discriminatory practices of the P.T.C. and P.R.T. employees union." They also drafted a petition demanding an end to the PTC's discriminatory policies. "The time has come," the document read, "to put into practice the principles of democracy in American life, including employment practices in American industry. We ask that employment . . . be based solely upon merit and ability, regardless of color, race or creed." The protestors sent their petition to every black church and civic organization in the city in an attempt to arouse wider support. Their plan worked well: by October, the PTC campaign had gained such momentum that a throng of some twenty-five hundred people descended on city hall for another rally. Participants' signs read: "Jim Crow fights on Hitler's Side!" "Break up this Discrimination!" and "Stop PTC's Unfair Practice!" In front of the raucous assembly, Moore and other speakers stirred the crowd, repeatedly urging their listeners to make their voices heard. "[You must show your] indignation against the failure of public officials to intervene on behalf of

Negro workers," Moore implored her listeners. "We want equality, period: social equality, economic equality, and all the equality there is. Anyone who wants anything less isn't a man," Marshall Shephard told the crowd to roaring applause.[13]

People at the meeting were so aroused that they issued two resolutions, each of which revealed the political implications of the PTC fight. The first went to the FEPC. "[We express] righteous indignation," it read, "at the unfair labor policy of the Philadelphia Transit Company which undermines the morale of the Negro people, hampers the war effort and prolongs the war. In the spirit of democracy we demand that you order the PTC to desist from such unfair labor practices." In this resolution, black Philadelphians made clear their ties to and expectations of the federal government. Not only did they count on the FEPC to correct the company's unfair labor practices, they also demanded government action in support of their cause. After years of supporting Roosevelt and the Democratic Party, they went to the government not to ask for a favor, but to demand their rights.[14]

The second resolution went to Mayor Samuel and by building on a months-long campaign to get his support was even more pointed in its political ramifications. Moore had pressed the PTC workers' case to the mayor over the last couple of months, writing a number of letters to Samuel asking him to publicly state his and the city's position on the PTC, but she never received a reply. As a result, the protestors at the October meeting issued a resolution to the mayor showing their discontent with his silence. At the outset they reminded Samuel, who was in the midst of his campaign against Bullitt, of their political clout. "Two thousand Philadelphia voters," the document read, "expressed the opinion that your . . . failure to take [a] forthright position on the issue invites a feeling of lack of confidence in your . . . leadership; we demand, therefore, that you immediately . . . order the Philadelphia Transit Company to begin to train and hire Negro men and women at once."[15]

Samuel ignored the petition, and a few days later Moore led a committee to his office. The mayor, well known for his failure to back black rights, refused to see them for an hour and a half and then feigned ignorance of their agenda. Moore reminded the mayor that she had written to him about the PTC for the past six months, to which Samuel only blandly responded that he would take the matter up later. "It [is] most unfair," he said, "to insist upon immediate action by the Mayor just prior to an election." With his comment, Samuel revealed how much black Philadelphians had learned about political activism. They had not only petitioned the mayor, they were also bringing pressure to bear in his most vulnerable moment. The NAACP, as the election results showed, could not guarantee retribution against the mayor for his intransigence, but activists were certainly willing to suggest the possibility. In refusing to tackle the matter until after the election, Samuel may well have feared an electoral backlash from Euro-Americans. They had shown their desire to keep blacks out of better PTC jobs, and for the mayor to back down would certainly infuriate many voters. At any rate, the committee, having gotten Samuel to promise to address the matter, backed off but vowed to return if Samuel failed them. "We are determined," Fauset told the press, "to leave no stone unturned in our campaign to establish a democratic system of hiring in the PTC."[16]

A week later, Moore, Fauset, and the rest of black Philadelphia made it clear they would not back down. More than a thousand people, responding to NAACP posters that urged "Believers in True Democracy" to "Mobilize for Action Now!," marched through the streets, demanding that the PTC end its discriminatory policies. The march went from South Philadelphia to city hall, where protesters voiced their anger right under the mayor's window. "The destiny of America is involved" in this fight, said Reverend E. Luther Cunningham. "We are fighting for equality of job opportunities and we are going to crack PTC." We will "throw a picket line around the PTC office this week and keep it there until company executives decide to practice this democracy there has been so much talk about," Moore told the crowd. "We don't intend to let up until colored men and women are given equal job opportunities." Democracy, equality, opportunity: these were the protestors' catchwords throughout a PTC campaign they believed was just an extension of the fight for equal rights they had been waging for many years.[17]

A number of groups recognized the fairness of black claims and came together to support the campaign. Left-wingers offered some of the most vocal aid, with the Communist Party's Jules Abercauph sending PTC management a formal letter of protest, urging the company to hire African Americans. He also sent a copy to Samuel but told the press he did not expect any action on the mayor's part. "Samuel, a front for the reactionary GOP Pew-machine has been a yes-man to the GOP bosses for years," he said. "And everyone knows how Pew with his Jim Crow record at his own ship yard stands on the question of racial discrimination." A few months later the *Daily Worker* put together a program to protest PTC discrimination. It included Arthur Huff Fauset and Abercauph as well as U.S. Communist Party chair William Z. Foster and numerous CIO leaders. NAACP leadership, always leery of the far left, cautiously accepted the support but worried that the Communists' actions might "divide the NAACP." Joseph Rainey, a future

In 1943, black Philadelphians carried out a series of demonstrations protesting the Philadelphia Transportation Company's racist employment practices. For them, the PTC's policies highlighted America's racial hypocrisy during World War II. Courtesy of Temple University Libraries, Urban Archives, Philadelphia PA.

NAACP president, expressed the thinking of most Philadelphians though. "In the present PTC fight the more the merrier," he wrote. "If the Communists have interested themselves in the cause of the Negro in this fight for better jobs on the local traction company, they certainly have interested themselves in a worthwhile project."[18]

The NAACP showed less ambivalence in soliciting and accepting Jewish support, actions that highlighted the fact that increasingly blacks and Jews were becoming the core of liberal Democratic strength in the city. "American principles of freedom and equal justice," Moore said in one speech, "cannot survive in the midst of growing anti-Semitic and anti-Negro feeling unless every decent American becomes active in the fight against such forces." Other NAACP leaders also expressed their belief in the links between racism and anti-Semitism and argued that the city needed a stronger black-Jewish alliance. Support came readily from the American Jewish Congress, which represented over two hundred Jewish groups, and the Anti-Defamation

Council. "Hiring on the basis of ability to do the job, without regard to race, creed, color or national origin, would give Philadelphia a transportation system in keeping with the American principle of equal opportunity for which our millions of soldiers are now fighting," wrote the American Jewish Congress. In part Jewish groups offered their support out of genuine abhorrence of discrimination against blacks. But they also knew that the PTC employed very few Jews (a later study found that Jews made up less than 1 percent of the workforce in the city's utilities), and they believed that this campaign might break down walls for them as well. With support growing in different quarters, African Americans were able to present PTC management with a petition bearing nearly thirteen thousand signatures calling for the end of discrimination at the company. This coalition that the NAACP was building, which represented the core of liberal politics in the city with its black, Jewish, and leftist constituencies, had real strength, but it could not end Jim Crow at the PTC alone.[19]

The FEPC

For help, black Philadelphians turned to the FEPC, which after months of local activism had decided to take up the PTC case. Longtime transit company workers, such as Maxwell Windham, had been filing complaints with the federal agency and demanding action since early 1943. Windham, who had received a note in his pay envelope inviting all PTC employees to enroll in the bus and trolley driver trainee program, told the FEPC that a company official had rejected him out of hand. When Windham asked why, the manager responded, "We are not hiring any colored [because of] an understanding between the officers of the Company and myself." Other workers reported similar conversations to the FEPC and the NAACP, which led Moore to demand action from the government agency. "We are calling [the PTC situation] to your attention," she wrote to the committee, "in order that some definite action might be taken within the very near future. . . . We shall appreciate hearing from you . . . within the next few days."[20]

The FEPC soon offered its help and proved to be a valuable ally. The committee opened a Philadelphia office in August 1943 with G. James Fleming in charge. Fleming, a member of a prominent local black family, had impeccable credentials for the post, having worked for the *Philadelphia Tribune*, written a manuscript for Gunnar Myrdal's *An American Dilemma*, and served on the FEPC since its inception. He forged a close relationship with Moore, letting her know the FEPC's plans ahead of time, and offered the community a reassuring presence backed by the strength of the federal government. Moore and Fleming urged people to use the FEPC, and in its first two months of operations the Philadelphia office registered over two dozen complaints against the transit company. Based on this testimony, Fleming held separate meetings with management and the PRTEU in early October 1943. PTC officials, bowing to local and federal pressure—but also knowing that the PRTEU would hold firm—agreed to employ blacks as drivers so long as they were acceptable to their fellow workers. Fleming, like PTC management, knew this would never happen but met with the PRTEU anyway. At that meeting Frank Carney and Frank Cobourn, the president and secretary-treasurer of the union, told Fleming they had nothing against black promotions but that their contract barred African Americans from any new jobs unless the PRTEU and PTC agreed to a change. They then admitted that tight employment conditions in Philadelphia might "necessitate a change" but argued that they could promise nothing until they had consulted with their delegates, many of whom were overseas. Fleming knew that the company and the union were manipulating him and would never give in, so he referred the matter to the national FEPC.[21]

Over the next two months FEPC chairman Malcolm Ross placed the weight of the federal government behind black promotions. In two November 5 meetings he got PTC management and PRTEU leaders to agree to a list of damning facts which demonstrated that management refused to employ African Americans as drivers because of their race, that in doing so they violated Executive Order 9346 (which had revised the FEPC's foundational Executive Order 8802), and that neither group could legally continue to use their contract to bar black promotions. Ross then ordered the company to cease all discriminatory practices and to file monthly reports proving it was living up to its legal obligation. He also ordered the PRTEU to accept black drivers without equivocation. While management agreed to obey the FEPC's directives, PRTEU leaders balked, accepting the facts of the case as Ross laid them out but arguing that they had to meet with their delegates before agreeing to follow the orders. Ross granted the union leaders time to hold a meeting but warned that the findings of fact and the directives would be final in ten days unless the committee heard any objections in that time.[22]

Carney and Cobourn quickly mobilized their union against the FEPC ruling. In a series of meetings, they convinced most of their members to protest the committee's directives and to demand a public hearing. Their stand, with management having backed down, made them look like the sole opponents of black promotions even though company leaders had taken an equally racist position for decades. A petition from subway and elevated train drivers showed the widespread support for Carney's and Cobourn's views. "[We] do hereby Disagree with the Order of the Presidents Committee of Fair Employment Practices in Washington," the petition read. "We believe . . . The Philadelphia Transportation Company . . . is not Discriminating in any way. . . . The Company should have the right to Employ whoever they think best for these Positions. . . . Any change that the Fair Employment Committee has ordered would surely cause a Major Dissatisfaction to the Public and the Employes and [would] most likely lead to a Very Serious Situation." This petition, through which PTC workers began to build their case against black promotions, foreshadowed conservative critiques about government "interference" in the workplace that became widely popular in the future. The FEPC, they argued, was an outside meddler from the federal government trying to force the company to make hires not in its best interest. The committee had no right, moreover, to interfere in a local company's affairs and doing so would only create strife in the city. And finally, the public and employees who found black promotions disturbing deserved as much if not more respect for their views than African Americans did. In some ways they ventured the argument that while the FEPC represented black rights, no one looked after the "rights" of white drivers, patrons, or management. Of course whites had constructed the entire discriminatory system and needed no one to look after their "rights." Such arguments about "government interference" and "employers' rights," whatever their superficial merit, masked a racist attempt to preserve "white" jobs. In the end, the drivers' racialized view of the world put drivers on the side of management and its prerogatives as opposed to the federal government and race-neutral employment.[23]

White drivers demanded a hearing with the FEPC, and on December 8 they got the chance to make their arguments. A standing-room-only crowd of four hundred spectators, many of them African Americans, crammed into the hearing room in city hall to take in the testimony. What they heard from the PRTEU leaders made many murmur in disapproval. From the start the PRTEU's Cobourn made it clear that his union found the FEPC's actions unjust. "The P.R.T. Employees' Union righteously complains that it is the victim of discrimination," Cobourn told the committee. His union was only following nationally accepted practices in the transit industry, he said, and it was being unfairly "singled out for the attention of the President's Committee on Fair Employment Practices." What really angered the workers, he continued, was that they "were being forced into something, without [their] consent." This kind of federal control over local practices was an unfair (he would later say unconstitutional) use of governmental power, and the workers had to stop this erosion of their rights. Cobourn also argued that by issuing the directive, government officials were callously ignoring seniority, one of the most valued rights of working people. "Compliance with the Committee's Directive," Cobourn said, "would disturb seniority and affect the transfer conditions of all employees." This line of argument provided a way for the PRTEU to connect with workers who did not subscribe to its racist policies. Interfering with seniority, it asserted time and again, would harm every hard-working driver in the PTC. In addition, any changes would give "seniority rights and job advancements . . . to outsiders and strangers in preference to employees who are protecting our homes and our freedoms in this critical period in our Nation's history," the union argued. The PRTEU's stand, then, might seem discriminatory toward blacks on the surface but in reality was an honorable attempt to preserve the jobs of those who were sacrificing everything overseas. At least that is what PRTEU leaders argued publicly. Most of their followers, however, knew that the real issue was black promotions. "Well, I thought the niggers was goin' to take away our seniority," one man told *PM*. Ross understood the traction this argument could gain and repeatedly told PRTEU members that his ruling would not affect seniority. But union leaders knew the fear PTC workers had of losing their jobs to black competitors and kept using the issue to paint the federal government as antagonistic to the white working class.[24]

Cobourn concluded his argument by charging that the FEPC's "unfair" directive and its attack on white workers' rights backed the employees into a corner and left them few options. The government's order was a "tragic mistake" in Cobourn's terms and could only lead to "chaos." The crowd, with the recent Detroit riots in mind, gasped when Cobourn made this threat, but he refused to back down. "Will you tell us," one FEPC member asked, "what you have got in mind, or what the Union members have in mind?" "I couldn't tell you what the Union members have in mind," Cobourn responded, but added that "they would not at this time accept such a radical change." Ross, knowing such statements were dynamite, warned Cobourn that "chaos was not inevitable" and that "all parties involved must share the responsibility for preventing any such hindrance to the war effort."[25]

Ross's warning that everyone must protect the war effort fit with his and most of the Roosevelt administration's overall view of the FEPC's role, a view that demonstrated the difference between white liberal and black conceptions of the government's place in fighting racism. On the one hand, Ross was an advocate of ending discrimination in the country's workforce, telling the PRTEU that Executive Order 8802 did not "declare a policy" but, rather, "reaffirmed what is and has been our national policy for more than three-quarters of a century." On the other hand, he believed that racial discrimination was fundamentally "a labor problem," not a moral or political one, for the FEPC. He knew his committee could not defeat Jim Crow single-handedly, and it was not his job to try. Instead, he had to fight workplace segregation when it hampered the war effort. The greatest problem with the PTC's Jim Crow policies, he told PRTEU leaders, was that "a truly great proportion of our manpower would be lost to the war effort." That Attorney General Francis Biddle agreed with Ross showed that the FEPC chairman's thinking was commonly held. "Emphasis of the Committee," Biddle told the president, "should be on preventing discrimination against workers as a problem of manpower, presenting it as a national need for full employment in the war." This stance was in some ways a shrewd move, drawing on the patriotism of America's workers and the urgent needs of the home front to encourage acceptance of the FEPC's orders. But it worried many advocates of black equality that the FEPC, not to mention the government in general, might not remain so steadfast in times of peace. "I am confident," Fellowship of Reconciliation leader James Bristol wrote to A. J. Muste, that such an approach "is trying to build racial equality on sand rather than on rock, that it is opportunistic and expedient but will not prove enduring." Those were prescient words that well captured the federal government's too-often ambivalent support of black rights.[26]

Despite this limited commitment, African Americans believed that the FEPC offered them the best chance to gain workplace access, and they used the PTC hearings to stake their claim. The NAACP's Moore made the case most forcefully, arguing that the company's discrimination harmed America's war effort and, more important, damaged the very democracy for which the nation was fighting. "Discrimination, in time of war, is treason and we should stand shamed before the world were we to permit it," she said of the PTC's practices. "Democracy is not merely a word. . . . It stands for equality of opportunity for every man to work and make a living for himself and his family. . . . Negroes are employed on the Transportation systems of a number of our larger cities . . . [so] why, in the City of Brotherly Love is there no brotherly love?" Other groups, especially leftist unions and Jewish organizations supported the NAACP's claims. "Your order is a step forward in making democracy work for the colored people," wrote the Leather Workers Union. "The workers of Local 30 support your committee wholeheartedly." Dozens of individuals offered their support of African American goals as well. "The deaths and tragedies of war," one woman wrote, "won't have served a God-

workers, meant the right of the majority to discriminate, not the right of everyone to have an equal opportunity in the workplace.[29]

The government, PTC workers believed, rejected their views because of black political power. With black votes critical to the Democratic Party and African Americans getting at least occasional support from Democratic leaders, many white workers believed that the party in power ignored their desires or at best took their votes for granted. "The whole thing is politics," one man said. "They went down to Washington and forced their way in." If the government would just listen, the strikers believed, they could make a compelling case for maintaining segregation at the PTC. But they were constantly rebuffed. At different times McMenamin met with the War Manpower Commission's McNamee and General Hayes, but each time the officials told him there was nothing to discuss. Equal opportunity was now government policy, and white workers could not alter it. These dismissals angered the workers more than anything. All the men wanted, the strike committee claimed, was "a fair and just hearing," but none was offered. "There was no cooperation," the committee asserted, and "PTC men felt very sour because they believed they [had not] gotten justice." At one rally after another strikers echoed this theme, claiming that the government was "selling [them] down the river," to satisfy its black constituency. Such statements often brought back chants of "The hell with Roosevelt!" "The Civil War freed the blacks from the whites," cried one man, and "we need another Lincoln to free the whites from the blacks."[30]

Many white Philadelphians shared the strikers' distaste for federal intervention in local affairs. This was certainly not the case when it came to home loans, WPA jobs, and employment paid for by war contracts, but people understood that the PTC intervention was intimately connected to black rights, and their subsequent attacks on the administration showed how racism was sapping liberalism from below. The blame for all the race problems, one man wrote, belongs on "the New Deal social agencies that are trying to revolutionize the mode of living and working of the Philadelphia public by their constant meddling in the affairs of others. . . . The issue is . . . the right of the citizen to be let alone versus New Deal regimentation." If the government has the right to dictate people's lives like this, wrote another man, then America should "bring Hitler in as the next Vice President. The job should be right up his alley." Other writers echoed these themes of government coercion, disastrous New Deal meddling, and the dwindling rights of white Americans under the Roosevelt administration. The acerbic conservative columnist Westbrook Pegler put it succinctly. "The same authorities who decry discrimination," he wrote, "[now] discriminate against white Americans." With such feelings growing daily, interracial unity in the Democratic Party, to the extent it ever existed, was in trouble.[31]

Although PTC workers directed their anger at the federal government in general, the FEPC took special abuse. "The FEPC," Cobourn said, is "trying to set a match to a powder keg. . . . There is much unrest here and in other cities, and the FEPC is trying to capitalize on it to bring about social reforms by law, instead of letting things work out gradually by themselves." A father of two boys who wanted jobs in the transit company after finishing their tours-of-duty overseas drew the connections explicitly between FEPC activism, Democratic politics, and black demands. Tellingly, he highlighted the FEPC's role at the start of his letter. "I was very well pleased to read in today's paper where the P.T.C. Union defied the F.E.P.C. order to hire Negroes," he wrote. "Thank God the P.T.C. does not have to depend on the Nigger vote like the politicians are doing in Philadelphia. . . . When you Niggers try to force your way into private industry, you are asking for trouble and you will sure as hell get it. Hats off to the P.T.C. Union, they showed you niggers how the rank and file white people feel toward you."[32]

Newspapers and politicians across the South seconded this view of the FEPC. Editors from Dallas, Savannah, and Charleston blasted the committee for the way it implemented its "arbitrary and inept policies" in Philadelphia. No one, however, vented more anger at the committee than Georgia senator Richard Russell. Russell's stance, which was unsurprising since he had opposed the Roosevelt administration for over a decade, reveals the similarity between conservative southern Democrats and northern white workers, both of whom moved in large numbers to the Republican Party in subsequent years. "The tragic strike," Russell said in a Senate speech, "was deliberately precipitated by . . . the so-called Fair Employment Practice Committee . . . [which wants] to refashion this country to conform to the ideas of its radical members." These "starry-eyed professional reformers," he continued, "mistreated" the PTC workers so badly that they had no choice but to strike. The government, moreover, had blatantly disregarded their just claims as it kowtowed to African Americans. The PTC workers "saw their humble petitions to the Congress of the United States . . . ignored," the senator claimed. "There was no agency of Government to hear them make their contentions. . . . There was no appeal from the decision of the F.E.P.C." And the committee's overwhelming power, Russell argued, made matters even worse. "When the F.E.P.C. press the button they throw into action every agency of the Federal Government," he said. It is "not only the most powerful but the most ruthless agency of the entire Government." The situation reminded him of Reconstruction, when the federal government "imposed" its will "upon the southern people." Russell closed with a warning to the president about the "dangers" he believed federal power presented to local rights, the bedrock, in his view, of America's democracy. "This F.E.P.C. is the most dangerous force in existence in the United States today," he said. "It is a greater threat to victory than 50 fresh divisions enrolled beneath Hitler's swastika or the setting sun of Japan."[33]

In his speech Russell crystallized the opposition to the FEPC and government intervention in general. Although he argued from a southern perspective that drew on the "horrors" of Reconstruction and the damage that federal power had wrought on his region, many of his comments could have come just as easily from the mouths of PTC workers. Russell and the trolley drivers ignored the transparent weaknesses of the FEPC and the federal government's ambivalent commitment to black rights, arguing to the contrary that the committee wielded unlimited power and ran roughshod over white Americans. There was no government organization, they believed, to address white workers' grievances. Instead, everyone concentrated on black claims, which left whites with a strike as their only option. Pressing workers this way endangered not only the war effort, but peaceful race relations across the nation. If the FEPC continued with its methods, national unity would fracture, the war could be lost, and so could the peace. The strike, to southern politicians and Philadelphia trolley drivers, was about more than the PTC; it was about standing up to the "dangers" of federal power and fighting for local rule. At heart, "local rule" meant a racialized democracy that valued white prerogatives over minority rights or equal opportunity. William Fogg, the driver who presented the petition to the Smith Committee, agreed wholeheartedly with Russell's comments and thought his co-workers would too. "Your speech," he told the senator, "covers all the phases of this strike very clearly and places the blame and responsibility where it belongs. . . . I would like to know if you could send me 10,000 copies of your speech as I would like to place this speech in the hands of every Philadelphia Transportation Co. Employee. We . . . sure appreciate your efforts in trying to defeat the F.E.P.C."[34]

Black and Liberal Views

People who believed in an expansive, egalitarian democracy disagreed with the strikers and Russell and focused on the strike's meaning for the fair employment committee and for the nation's future more generally. Locally and nationally, commentators argued that the transit strike offered a prime example of why America had to buttress the FEPC. The lesson of the strike, the *Nation* asserted, was that the FEPC needed to have "full statutory recognition, with power to enforce its decisions." The *New York Post* agreed, adding that a permanent FEPC backed by federal law would make white workers think twice before staging such a strike again. But the transit workers did have legitimate fears, the editors cautioned. Workers well remembered the hard times of the Depression and rightly worried that massive unemployment would return after the war. The nation, the *Post* wrote, needed a permanent Fair Employment Practices Committee, but Congress also needed to pass a Full Employment Bill to assure all workers that they would have jobs once the war was over. If the government failed to act, the paper warned, the nation could expect more racial conflict in the years ahead. Just such a bill became part of President Roosevelt's Economic Bill of Rights, but an increasingly conservative Congress refused to pass the legislation.[35]

Black commentators agreed that the strike proved the need for a permanent FEPC but expanded their arguments to take on all forms of discrimination. For Arthur Huff Fauset, the transit strike was "the test of the FEPC." "The Negro people wait patiently," he asserted, "but not too patiently. . . . If there is no equity now . . . they have even less hope for equity once the war emergency has been safely passed." Others made the links between the FEPC, black equality, and true democracy even more explicit. "Congress," an NNC leader insisted, "must give permanent status and adequate authority to [the FEPC to ensure] war jobs may be open to all without discrimination, and it must adopt legislation to abolish the polltax and end Jimcrowism in all other areas of our social life." Groups including the local NAACP, the Council for Equal Job Opportunity, and the Jewish Community Relations Council put these ideas into practice, drafting FEPC legislation for Philadelphia and the state government before the year was out. "We believe," wrote the Jewish council under the headline "Job Opportunity," "that a community cannot be discrimination-minded toward Negroes and democratic-minded toward other racial or religious groups." The FEPC, in this view, made an important statement about American democracy while opening opportunities for Jews as well as African Americans.[36]

Beyond the FEPC, opponents of the strike were of two minds about how to think about the walkout. For some, the strike highlighted the hypocrisy of discriminating against African Americans in the midst of a war for democracy. Far from a racist monolithic bloc, many whites, particularly those in Jewish, leftist, and CIO organizations, exhibited this strain of thinking. For many others, however, racial equality held little appeal. They worried more about the strike's effect on the war effort than anything else. People with such views demanded the end of the strike and the promotion of African Americans at the PTC, but their rationale would evaporate at war's end. At that point, they could as easily side with people like the PTC strikers as they could with those who wanted racial equality. This second line of thinking bolstered the black cause during the war but offered a shaky foundation for the pursuit of long-term gains.

For many people, black service in World War II entitled African Americans to equal treatment at home. As one man wrote, "If the Negro is good enough to die for me on the battlefront, he is good enough to drive for me in Philadelphia." In fact, for many people equality of opportunity, democracy for all, was the reason America was fighting the war. For people holding this view, backing down in this strike, admitting that certain Americans did not deserve equal treatment, undermined the country's democratic principles. "Compromise," wrote the *New York Times*, "would be indecent." An FEPC lawyer asserted that any wavering by the government would be even worse than that; it would mean that "we are suspending the Declaration of Independence and the Bill of Rights." Many Philadelphians agreed with these sentiments. "Over there," wrote one woman, "where the blood of white and black men flows in a common stream for a common cause—Democracy— they might well ask, where is this Democracy for which we die?" Democracy clearly held a different meaning for these Philadelphians than it did for the strikers and their supporters.[37]

Groups on the left along with Jewish organizations made the importance of the strike to America's polity particularly clear. Organizations from the Communist Party and the NNC to the National Maritime Union and the Mine, Mill, and Smelter Workers' Union all lauded the government's stance in the strongest terms. To them, federal intervention not only meant equity at the PTC, it also heralded, in the words of a Mine, Mill writer, a "future when our government, coming closer and closer to the fullest democratic people's government, may well move in other areas to enforce the constitutional rights of the Negro people." "No retreat," added the TWU, "is possible in the forward march of the people, the government and labor against Jimcrow." Jewish groups largely voiced their concern because they found the transparent racism of the transit strike abhorrent. "Philadelphia stands disgraced before the nation," a Jewish veterans' organization told Mayor Samuel and Governor Martin, "if irresponsible elements are permitted to continue to cripple our transportation system at a time when all Americans—white, Negro, Catholic, Jew and Protestant—are giving up their lives on the battlefield to insure full equality for all of our citizens." Of course these groups were also looking out for themselves, fearing that racial discrimination would lead to anti-Semitism. "[We believe that] white vs. Negro or Negro vs. white feeling . . . leads to anti-Semitism," wrote the American Jewish Congress, "and that the present strike situation is a preview of what is going to happen in the post-war period with respect to the employment of veterans." Whatever their motivations, Jewish groups overall offered strong support to the cause of nondiscrimination and, combined with support from the left, showed how a multiracial, black-Jewish-left alliance remained a pillar of Philadelphia's liberal politics.[38]

The other strain of thought opposed to the strike, based solely on the need to promote the war effort, suggested a far less promising future for interracial liberalism. Proponents of this view argued that black equality was not the paramount issue and that squabbles over rights could be "negotiated" in the future. Nowhere did they suggest that black rights represented a matter of principle for America's democracy; all that mattered was winning the war, and the transit strike had to end because it hampered that effort. "The major imperative is to get the cars, trains and buses running," wrote the *Inquirer* in an editorial representative of the city's white newspapers. "Philadelphians and the national war effort have suffered enough through this unspeakable P.T.C. walkout. It must be ended." The federal government may have inappropriately ordered the promotions, the editors continued, but "this is not the time to go into complicated negotiations dealing with racial and other issues. There will be time later for [that]." A slew of letters to the editor agreed. "Let's do first things first," wrote one man. "Get our transportation system rolling so our war workers can get to and from their work. . . . Discussion and settlement of controversial questions should be postponed until after the war is won."[39]

African Americans dismissed this view, arguing that there was nothing to negotiate, nothing to settle. Their country could either live up to its democratic promises or expose itself as a hypocritical defender of Jim Crow in a war against other proponents of master-race theories. In telegrams to Mayor Samuel, Governor Martin, and federal officials, including the president, NAACP leaders pressed authorities to "stand absolutely firm and refuse to yield to strikers . . . [because] the American Government cannot afford to yield to mob action to negate Democracy of this character." "Mr. President," one man asked just after the strike started, "will we ever have a true Democratic country? Will what has been printed in our constitution just be mere words? . . . Can we stop race discrimination?" A woman whose family had lost two young men overseas added a poignant appeal. "We who have lost boys have a right to expect something because of it," she wrote. "We sent them to the ends of the world to fight for this thing—and we don't seem to enforce it [at home]. The government has a right to stick to its guns in this issue, and let us know that they expect to insist on a better life for all because our boys have died for it."[40]

These demands for support showed that African Americans would not stand for government equivocation, and federal officials responded quickly. The situation "will be administered fairly," wrote War Manpower Commission head Paul McNutt to Walter White. "There is no question of yielding in [my] mind." It was a good thing too that the government supported black rights with military muscle, Arthur Huff Fauset and E. Washington Rhodes asserted. For if Roosevelt had backed down, Fauset wrote, riots "would have spread from Philadelphia to other cities [and] the Roosevelt administration would have been discredited." Rhodes agreed, saying that in Philadelphia "Hell would have broken loose." In the first couple days of the strike it nearly did, even with the quick federal backing.[41]

Philadelphia did not explode in racial violence like other war-era cities did, but it did witness enough conflict to make many people fear the dangers the strike had unleashed. The town felt "panicky," in the words of one black reporter, and Spaulding believed that "all the ingredients of a first class race riot were boiling and brewing." Local government officials canceled the Phillies' games, closed the city's bars, and warned white Philadelphians to stay out of black neighborhoods. North Philadelphia, by this time the site of racial change over many decades, bore the brunt of the violence. The police department estimated that 80 percent of the city's disturbances took place in these neighborhoods, which the *New York Times* labeled as the "borderline district." African Americans there threw coal at passing motorists, slashed the tires of parked cars, and smashed windows in some three hundred stores. The violence had a political edge, as blacks scrupulously avoided damaging those businesses known for fair practices while often singling out people of Irish and Italian descent for abuse. Rioters, for example, smashed the windows of the Ancient Order of Hibernians Lodge, and two women attacked Officer Theodore Martini and spit in his face. At the same time, African Americans reassured frightened Jewish merchants that they need not be scared. "We aren't going to hurt you none," several blacks told one man. "You haven't done anything to us; it's those damned transit fellers who think they're too good to work with us. They're our real enemies." The strike raised feelings for many that one person put into words: "I thought then and many times afterwards, how much and how far did they (the whites) feel they could push us? Did they not realize that the point beyond which no human being can go and maintain dignity was dangerously close? . . . In a matter of seconds every indignity suffered, every injustice or hurt received at the hands of whites flashed in kaleidoscopic rapidity through my mind. . . . I felt and knew I could kill easily, whom did not matter, just so the person was white."[42]

Although the climate was right for a massive racial clash, the actions of the police and black organizations and, most importantly, the arrival of federal soldiers kept the city relatively calm. The police knew how dangerous the situation was, and despite their poor relations with black Philadelphians they worked to keep the peace. Pleasantly surprised African Americans roundly praised officers for the "excellent and restrained job" they did in controlling the situation. Detroit even sent representatives from its police department to learn how to better handle such disturbances. At the same time, the NAACP and other black organizations sent members into the most troubled neighborhoods, urging people to remain calm. "Keep Your Heads and Your Tempers!" their fliers read. "This stoppage is a disgrace to Philadelphia, to America and to Democracy." Violence, they said, would solve nothing. Instead, people should wire the PTC and Mayor Samuel and demand that the company obey the government, which was standing firmly behind black promotions. In private messages, the NAACP warned Mayor Samuel and Governor Martin that events were getting beyond the organization's control and that if the local government failed to act, the association "could not be responsible for possible resultant action by embittered groups." In part, NAACP officials used the message of this telegram, with its implied threat of violence, to pressure officials to act. But the wire was also a response to the demands that association officials were getting from within their own community. Many young people told reporters that NAACP methods were "too slow" and that they wanted "this problem solved now, not later." "Our young people are in earnest," said one man. "They are not seeking trouble [but] if they are molested they will fight." Despite the threats, city officials did little to promote racial peace, which meant that the army arrived just in time.[43]

African Americans rejoiced when the federal government lived up to their expectations and used force to ensure black rights. Transit vehicles with soldiers aboard brought laughing, clapping crowds into the streets across North Philadelphia. "The Negroes in this section are satisfied now that Uncle Sam has taken over," said a black policeman. "They have confidence that

The worst violence of the PTC strike occurred in North Philadelphia. Most attacks had a political edge, focusing on shop owners known for discriminating against black residents. Courtesy of Temple University Libraries, Urban Archives, Philadelphia PA.

things will work out without them getting shoved around, now that Washington" was involved. The NNC, the Urban League, and local black leaders such as Arthur Huff Fauset all offered their thanks to the federal government and the CIO as well. "Aren't you proud of our great President!" Fauset wrote. "And of the mighty CIO! Suppose either had faltered. Every gain made in recent years would have been lost. The FEPC would be a dead letter; trade unionism among Negroes would pass away like a summer's breeze." No one was happier than the eight recently promoted drivers who always believed the government would compel Philadelphians to observe the principle of nondiscrimination. They all told reporters that they thought of themselves as pioneers and that, with the government's help, they would make it. Their "implicit faith" in the government, as one reporter put it, led them to believe that federal authorities would "take swift action to guarantee [their] rights."

It took years of campaigning and ultimately federal intervention, but African Americans finally received driving jobs at the PTC in 1944. Here James Stewart receives instruction from William Poisell as Stewart trains to become a transit driver. Courtesy of Temple University Libraries, Urban Archives, Philadelphia PA.

Some African Americans still wondered, however, what the strike said about American society in the midst of World War II. The wife of one of the new black drivers, after telling a reporter that her husband had served nine months in the South Pacific, was unsure that her husband's "sacrifice was worth it." When the strike ended a few days later and African Americans began taking trolleys out on their runs, most of the city's blacks would have told her that indeed it was.[44]

The Strike and National Politics

Black commentators in the strike's aftermath pointed to the president's actions in support of black rights and the FEPC as the reason to back FDR and the Democratic Party in the presidential election of 1944. As observers drew the connections between jobs, black opportunity, and federal authority, the strike blended almost seamlessly into formal politics. Many African Americans believed that federal power, as wielded by the president, offered the most effective strategy for attacking discrimination. "The prompt action of the government in support of the FEPC," wrote one editor, shows "that Franklin D. Roosevelt still stands for freedom and democracy and that his continuation in office for another four years is the only way by which the Negro can consolidate the social gains under the New Deal." The Republicans, many pundits believed, were guilty of unleashing the ugly racism raised in the strike, and African Americans would remember that come November. The attitude of Mayor Samuel and Governor Martin would be "marked and noted by Negro Republicans throughout the country," said a New York politician, who then attacked GOP presidential candidate Thomas Dewey for his "utter indifference to what happened in Philadelphia."[45]

Other groups agreed with this assessment of the GOP and urged their members to support the president and, by extension, African Americans and the Democratic Party at the polls. In their charges, they showed they understood the political tactics the Republicans were learning to employ. "The Republican high command," the TWU said, "hoped to use this strike for the purpose of disuniting the people and to prevent the re-election of President Roosevelt." At the same time, the editors of the *Daily Worker* asked their readers, "Who would profit by such a disturbance? Who would want to embarrass the Roosevelt administration by presenting it with such an ugly business?" Mayor Samuel and the Republicans, that's who, answered myriad groups ranging from the CIO and the Federated Press to Philadelphia's Democratic leaders and the Fellowship of Reconciliation. "Many of [the top strikers] are also local Republican ward heelers who have worked for the Pew machine for many years," reported the Federated Press, and they wanted "to put Pres. Roosevelt on the spot." CIO leaders blamed "partisan industrialists" and distributed fliers urging people to "Register Now So You Can Vote in November." And army investigators, no friends of the *Daily Worker* or the CIO, argued that the strike's instigators were trying to discredit the FEPC, the War Manpower Commission, and the administration in general. All observers noted how the Republicans were encouraging, even guiding, the racial politics of the strike. "Certain conservative business and political circles did not object to nor do anything to stop the strike," Walter White observed, because "if federal authorities . . . failed to take an unequivocal stand, Negro votes would be alienated, while the taking of an unequivocal stand would alienate white votes."[46]

Politics seldom works as mechanically as White suggested, but his statement revealed the kernel of Republican thinking that became more obvious in the weeks before the election and even more so in years to come. Politics, in this view, was a zero-sum game in which federal support for African Americans automatically alienated white working-class voters. White was not the only one who saw the danger: Attorney General Francis Biddle had warned Roosevelt of this kind of racial politics a year earlier. It was important to back the FEPC, Biddle believed, because otherwise, the administration would lose its black supporters. But pushing for change too vigorously, particularly from Washington, would inflame whites against the president. "Results," Biddle wrote, "should be achieved by negotiation and persuasion locally, through men of local standing, with only occasional use of public hearings or application of sanctions." "Public pressures arousing race emotions," he emphasized, "should be avoided."[47]

In the wake of the strike, conservatives found it easy to connect federal power, black rights, and electoral support of the Roosevelt administration. In doing so, they continued to build an elite-grassroots coalition loyal to the GOP. Republican leaders did not focus exclusively on race, but with the strike as backdrop, the implications of "federal power" were obvious to everyone. By late August, PTC officials started a whispering campaign to make it clear to workers that the company had been "forced to follow the policy of upgrading Negroes because of dictation from Washington." At the same time, PTC workers circulated hundreds of cards reading "Franklin to Eleanor: You kiss the niggers and I'll kiss the Jews; And we'll stay in the White House as long as we choose." The defense attorney for the handful of arrested strike leaders warned the press that people wielding federal power were trying "to change the existing form of government to one closely resembling totalitarianism . . . [with authority] centralized in Washington." This thinking about centralized power, Washington's control of Philadelphia's local practices, and federal support for blacks and Jews spread throughout the city. The Italian *South Philadelphia American*, for example, showed how much its readership was moving away from the president by calling him the "Great I Am" and charging that he wanted to monopolize the White House and take control of the country. "Dictatorship," in the editors' view, was on the rise in America, and "only the election of Dewey [could] squelch it." Week after week, they blasted the "meddling bureaucrats" and "long-haired professors" of the administration and the "Russian methods" of the CIO. "Vote Republican and Save the Republic," was their final call two days before the election. Irish newspapers in Kensington and elsewhere followed suit, decrying the growth of federal power and the coercion it brought while mostly avoiding overt references to race. But the underlying issue of race was always there, and occasionally it surfaced, as in a Republican campaign brochure that circulated in Irish and Italian West Philadelphia warning people that "black domination" threatened to destroy their city. "Dear Neighbor," the pamphlet read. "Will you stand by and see our homes, schools and our entire neighborhood taken away from you and your children by a race stimulated by RUM—JAZZ—WAR-EASY MONEY? The slum shocked NEGRO whose motto is 'Jesus will lead me and the welfare feed me.' Vote a straight Republican Ballot next Tuesday and save your salvation."[48]

Such views in the Italian and Irish communities contrasted with the thinking in Jewish and black areas, and the disparity troubled Democratic leaders. Where the Italian press blasted Roosevelt at every turn, the *Jewish Times* referred to him in reverential terms. "Abraham Lincoln was a miracle," one of its columnists wrote. "And we must have something of the same feeling as we contemplate Franklin D. Roosevelt. . . . If I were a mystic . . . I would say that in the entire career of F.D.R. the hand of God is to be seen." In part, Jews supported Roosevelt because of his prosecution of the war against Germany, but the *Jewish Times* was also the only ethnic newspaper to condemn the transit strike and to demand that the PTC hire people regardless of color or creed. It also supported federal intervention to stop racial and religious discrimination. It was, in fact, the only ethnic newspaper to pay any attention to the strike. The rest merely mentioned the shutdown in passing or acted as if it never happened—a glaring omission given that the walkout stopped the city for a week. The editors of the Italian and Irish newspapers may have decided to ignore the story since their readers had lost and there was nothing to gain from discussing the defeat. Whatever the case, the Republican offensive in the Irish and Italian communities, drawing on the issues raised by the transit strike, worried Democratic leaders enough that they complained to federal authorities that "the race issue has been fanned by Republican sources to discredit Roosevelt."[49]

Democrats found these maneuvers dangerous because many observers thought the election would be close. Gallup polls in early November showed Dewey well ahead in states that controlled eighty-five electoral votes while Roosevelt led in states with 165 electoral votes. Statistics for the densely populated industrial North, including Pennsylvania, Ohio, Illinois, New York, and Massachusetts, showed Roosevelt and Dewey within two points of each other. If a few of those states fell to Dewey, the Republicans could seize control of the White House. Pennsylvania loomed as one of the most important of those states, and pundits ranging from *Newsweek* and Columbia's

TABLE 2

Percentages of Selected Ethnic Groups Voting Democratic, 1936–44

	1936 (President)	1940 (President)	1943 (Mayor)	1944 (President)
Irish	59	58	45	43
Italian	69	60	34	43
Jewish	77	81	59	89
Black	62	63	46	68

Sources: Voting data drawn from Grove, "Decline of the Republican Machine"; Miller, "The Negro in Pennsylvania Politics"; Shover, "Ethnicity and Religion in Philadelphia Politics."

Bureau of Applied Social Research to the *Philadelphia Record* and the *Inquirer* believed that Pennsylvania could determine who the nation's next president would be. Philadelphia, in turn, would most likely determine Pennsylvania's choice. The transit strike, the statement it made about black rights and federal power, and the workers' reaction to that statement had profound ramifications for the upcoming presidential election. If enough white workers deserted Roosevelt, the Democrats could lose.[50]

Of course Roosevelt did win reelection in 1944 but by the narrowest margin in his four campaigns. His smashing triumph in the Electoral College by over three hundred votes obscured the fact that he only won about 52 percent of the popular vote. In Pennsylvania his race was particularly tight, as he won by only a hundred thousand ballots. Philadelphians offered the president stronger support than the rest of the state, giving him nearly three-fifths of their votes, but most of this advantage came in the black and Jewish communities. African Americans, who had heard for months that only Roosevelt would continue the work of the FEPC, gave the president over two-thirds of their vote. His name and image, according to several commentators, still held a "magic appeal" in the city's black neighborhoods. Jews gave the president even stronger support, some 89 percent of their vote. But the Italian and Irish districts showed a portentous willingness to desert the Democrats in the wake of the strike. Only 43 percent of the city's Italian Americans voted for Roosevelt, down from some 60 percent in 1940. Irish Americans, who had given the president 58 percent of their vote in 1940, similarly gave Roosevelt only 43 percent of their support. A tenuous interracial coalition that had formed in the mid-1930s in support of the president and his New Deal had cracked along racial lines. To be sure, there were still many liberal whites and Jews who joined African Americans to back the Democratic Party, but for many working-class whites, forming a cross-class racially conservative coalition within the GOP made more sense.[51]

Although the president won his fourth election and carried the city in 1944, his victory could not hide the weakening of white support for liberal politics. The federal government's forceful backing of black rights had shown African Americans that the Democratic administration offered the best avenue to equality. Without the FEPC, the army, and the president behind them, they could not have won their fight against Jim Crow at the PTC. Jews, much like African Americans, saw the importance of federal power in ending discrimination, and they also continued to support the president. But other groups, particularly Italian and Irish Americans, now understood that greater federal power did not guarantee what they believed was their right to control the people with whom they worked and lived. Their version of democracy, local majority rule free from federal regulation of racial matters, had lost in the transit strike, toppled by government intervention. These voters had supported Roosevelt during the Depression, when his programs improved their lives, but this looked like a wholly different Democratic Party to them: one oriented toward helping African Americans at the expense of white workers' prerogatives. With the Democratic Party seemingly allied with blacks, many Irish and Italian Philadelphians were willing to shift their allegiance, even to a Republican Party that had abandoned most of its political machine functions of helping working people and was now run by industrialists, such as Joseph Grundy and Joseph Pew.

In the coming years, the city's Republican Party, although dominated by business interests, attracted the support of much of Philadelphia's white working class. It did so by remembering the issues raised in the transit strike. The Republicans promoted themselves as the party opposed to "unfair" federal action, "disastrous" governmental programs, and "forced" black equality. They would stand between white homeowners, many of them in the new suburbs, and black public housing. They would stave off attempts to create city- and state-level FEPCs. They would craft an alliance by offering white voters an alternative to the liberal politicians who many felt had become too solicitous of black demands. In the end, they would champion a racialized politics that paid attention to, even promoted, white grievances, and they did so in 1948, not 1968.

Public housing became an even more racially and politically divisive issue in the 1950s. Many white Philadelphians, like these from Olney in 1956, believed that public housing meant black housing and that it constituted a threat to their communities. Republican politicians fostered such feelings as a means of fracturing Democratic constituents along racial lines. Courtesy of Temple University Libraries, Urban Archives, Philadelphia PA.

rather than serving as a force for integration, as Clark and Dilworth had hoped, reinforced the city's growing segregation. Most African Americans could not afford to move to the suburbs or were not allowed to live there, so they had to turn to rundown homes or public housing, which forced them to live in clusters in the central city. As Philadelphians equated public housing with black housing it lost whatever popular support it once had and became, in the words of the historian John Bauman, the government's "unloved step-child." Even more, people could not understand why the Democrats continued to support the program, and some turned on the party because of it. Jane Thorp, spokesperson for a northeast civic association, complained that the "social planners" were taking over and that many people in her neighborhood "believed that the NAACP was recruiting public housing tenants from the South and that the Dilworth administration wanted to place projects in strategic wards to fill them with black Democrats." People did not have to believe in conspiracy theories to know which party to support if they wanted to stop public housing, and Democrats were well aware of the political winds. Clark and Dilworth stood by public housing throughout their careers, but other Democratic stalwarts, such as Congressman William Green and John McDevitt, abandoned the program in favor of white homeowners. As many whites in the suburbs and the city—whether of Italian, Irish, Jewish, or old-stock European descent—turned on public housing because of racial concerns, they helped a Republican alliance coalesce.[40]

The Workplace

As the city's white population suburbanized so did its workplaces, and this only compounded the problems of black Philadelphians. In many ways the two issues reinforced each other. African Americans could not live in the suburbs where companies with the best jobs were relocating, and they soon found their incomes stagnating or disappearing. Without steady employment, many blacks found that government housing was the only place they could afford to live, which concentrated them even more within the inner city, where there were few jobs, and thus the cycle repeated itself over again. Housing and employment were not so much separate issues as mutually reinforcing problems that circumscribed the lives of the city's African Americans.

Blacks were not the only ones who faced employment problems in the immediate postwar period: all members of the city's working class dealt with trends that pulled jobs out of the city. Gladys Palmer, an astute observer of Philadelphia's labor market, warned as early as 1944 that the youngest and oldest workers, former housewives, and blacks would all face a tight job market as veterans resumed their careers. Munitions workers too would find their jobs cut as government contracts dried up, she predicted. Palmer was proven right when Baldwin Locomotive and Midvale Steel laid off half their employees, Sun Ship contracted from thirty-four thousand to four thousand workers, and Cramp's Shipyard closed its gates entirely. The Frankford arsenal, the naval yard, and other government installations also cut thousands of jobs. The end of federal money added to anxious feelings engendered by the slide of textiles and other local industries. In the early twentieth century, Philadelphia employed 4 percent of the nation's industrial workforce, but that number fell to only 2 percent by the end of World War II, and it kept falling. Textile manufacturers employed some 120,000 workers at the end of World War II, but by the early 1950s they were shifting their operations to the South to avoid higher labor costs, which caused Philadelphia to lose 91,000 jobs over the next four decades. At the same time, the city's industries as a whole, which had employed 350,000 people in 1950, lost 50,000 jobs by the end of the decade and another 200,000 by 1985. "The war," one historian accurately noted, "returned only an artificial prosperity to the region and did little to stem the underlying economic decline that had predated the Great Depression."[41]

While some of the lost jobs headed south, many moved to the suburbs. From 1919 to 1939, the city of Philadelphia held some 60 to 65 percent of the metropolitan area's manufacturing jobs, but that number fell to 50 percent in 1943. The slide worsened after the war to the point where, in 1980, fewer than four in ten jobs were within the city limits. The city's northeast and Montgomery and Bucks counties picked up the bulk of this work, as King of Prussia built an industrial park for SKF, General Electric, and other industries. At the same time, Yale & Towne, Budd, and B. F. Goodrich built new factories in the northeast. Boosters trumpeted this pattern of industrial growth as a new "frontier" on the "banks of the Delaware" and argued that suburban factories, with their lush landscaping and spacious parking lots, made good neighbors for new suburbanites. They also claimed that manufacturers had no choice but to move since their old locations in the heart of the city were "industrially blighted." Built along rivers and rail lines, nineteenth-century sources of power and transportation, these factories were "crowded, crumbling, dingy and scabrous structures" that made truck transport and plant expansion virtually impossible.[42]

In their rush to glorify the new postwar economic geography, boosters ignored the effect that job dispersal was having on working-class Philadelphians who did not want to leave the city. Those who refused to follow their employers to the suburbs found their salaries barely keeping pace with inflation, while residents of Bucks County and Montgomery County saw their pay rise by 46 and 26 percent, respectively, over the next couple decades. Stagnant wages and the dearth of jobs affected Philadelphia's newest immigrants, African Americans and later Hispanics, in particular because they seldom had the college education to take advantage of the growing number of white-collar jobs and could not live in the suburbs where manufacturers offered the steadiest factory work. The city, then, in the decade after World War II found itself on the verge of an urban crisis. People were losing their jobs, those who stayed employed had less income to spend at city stores, and the city had less tax revenue for streets, schools, and other services.[43]

While the dispersal of jobs and the long-term decline of the city's industry were troublesome developments, local union leaders, like those in other industrial centers, worried also about wages and contractual issues. They dealt with their concerns by joining a nationwide strike wave that hit industries ranging from steel and oil to electronics and meatpacking. In all, the nation lost some thirty million workdays to strikes in the last half of 1945 alone. In Philadelphia, eighty thousand workers walked out in the last months of 1944, with the largest number striking Baldwin Locomotive, Westinghouse, and General Electric. Workers from the AFL and CIO attended rallies together, carrying signs that asked, "Where's the promised 60 million jobs?" and declaring, "Full Employment is the Answer." Of all the strikes, that by the United Electrical Radio and Machine Workers of America at General Electric provoked the strongest reaction. Workers walked out there in mid-January 1946 and defied a court injunction that forbade picketing by more than ten people. On February 27, eight hundred strikers marched past the plant, and the police—displaying a far different attitude from just a year and a half earlier when the city's conservative establishment had backed the PTC strike—charged the crowd and beat the strikers with nightsticks. The next day, thirty-five hundred strikers and sympathizers marched near the plant, and again the police attacked, scattering the crowd. Word of the second attack spread through the city, and by noon thousands of CIO workers carrying signs that read "GE Cannot Run the City" had descended on city hall. Mayor Samuel heard threats of a general strike and arranged for talks between General Electric and its workers. Soon after, the company settled the conflict at its plants nationwide, agreeing to a pay raise of $1.48 a day, three-quarters of what its workers had demanded. Management later admitted, "There was little doubt who had won the strike," but it proved a Pyrrhic victory for organized labor.[44]

Over the next few years, corporate leaders reacted to the postwar strike wave by embarking on an antiunion offensive that deeply wounded the labor movement in Philadelphia and across the nation. Businessmen, as the historian Thomas Sugrue put it, "orchestrated an extraordinarily successful propaganda campaign that associated big business with 'true' American values, and tainted its critics with charges of communism. To challenge corporate policy was to risk political marginalization and disdain, and radical voices in the 1950s were muffled in the free enterprise crusade." A spate of national events, including rising Cold War tensions, passage of the Taft-Hartley Act, and the growth of McCarthyism gave further momentum to the corporate campaign. By the early 1950s, labor radicalism in Philadelphia had so faded into memory that the *Evening Bulletin* assured potential investors that the metropolitan area had "less labor trouble [than] almost any other

Working-class Philadelphians, who faced an uncertain future after World War II, staged a series of strikes highlighted by this one at General Electric in March 1946. While political and industrial leaders had condoned the PTC walkout, after the war they returned to the violent repression of strikes. The GE strikers shown here won concessions at the bargaining table but were ultimately unable to arrest Philadelphia's industrial slide. Courtesy of Temple University Libraries, Urban Archives, Philadelphia PA.

industrial area of the country. The big unions . . . operate under experienced and temperate leadership. Communism . . . has had hard going among Philadelphia's workers." Instead of organized labor's mass marches on city hall, a tour by the Freedom Train, with the Constitution, Declaration of Independence, and other relics from America's past, and an eleven-hour American Legion parade in 1949 symbolized Philadelphia's politics. The union movement had already passed its apex by the end of the 1940s, and despite a few victories it fell before a corporate onslaught and the right turn of the American public. Battered, labor could not slow Philadelphia's industrial slide. Just as important, one of the counterbalances to right-wing politics and one of the bastions of interracial liberalism, at least in the case of the CIO, lost its power.[45]

The failure of the labor movement, particularly the leftist CIO unions, to overcome larger structural economic problems spelled trouble for black workers. They had always faced discrimination in the city, but now with jobs disappearing African Americans had to compete with whites for an increasingly scarce resource. This competition led to greater discrimination by employers, racial conflicts, and deeper poverty for black Philadelphians. They tried to use racial advancement organizations, such as the NAACP and the Urban League, to arrest these trends, but often were overwhelmed by events.

The first years after World War II were filled with ominous signals for Philadelphia's black working class. African Americans had found employment at Sun Ship, the Pennsylvania Railroad, and the Philadelphia Transportation Company during the war, but their peak level of employment passed in July 1943. Many held onto their factory work, especially in metals, into the early 1950s, but as the war wound down and the government reduced its orders, companies laid off workers, and blacks were the first to go. In the first weeks after V-J Day in August 1945, Philadelphia companies fired some fifteen thousand black employees, most of whom found nothing but common labor or service work despite the industrial skills they had learned during the war. Studies showed that 75 percent of white males and 60 percent of white females held skilled or professional jobs, but only 35 percent of black males and 22 percent of black females were so employed. At the Richard Allen Homes, where 23 percent of the heads of household had worked in craft occupations in 1946, declining employment prospects and occupant turnover led by the early 1960s to only 6 percent holding those jobs. Such problems, in the words of one historian, "shattered the World War II illusion that Philadelphia's black population had at last found a secure job niche in manufacturing."[46]

Workplace discrimination, carried out by employers and often supported by white workers, confronted black Philadelphians at every turn. Newspapers routinely carried want ads asking for "whites only." The Commission on Law and Social Action, an American Jewish Congress affiliate, found that the number of help-wanted ads was dropping while discriminatory wording in the remaining ads was "showing a sharp increase in the Post-War period." A state survey in 1952 substantiated the commission's findings, reporting that one-third of Pennsylvania's companies discriminated against blacks in even the lowest, most unskilled positions. For supervisory, front office, or sales work, nearly 90 percent of the state's businesses admitted that they would not hire African Americans. This was, the commission wrote, a "barbaric rejection of our fellow citizens in a primary need." The commission's outrage brought little change, as black and white workers continued competing for the shrinking number of jobs.[47]

In the city's textile mills and metalworking shops, Euro-Americans clung to the jobs they saw disappearing around them. Particularly in stable working-class communities like Kensington, white claims on jobs often mixed with segregated housing to create explosive conflicts. Black newcomers in such neighborhoods, white residents believed, would not only harm their property values, they would also take their jobs. Social scientists found that those neighborhoods built on manufacturing income were particularly prone to racial violence as "weakened economic competitiveness" was transformed into "community solidarity and conflict." Black and interracial groups understood white fears about jobs and created organizations to highlight the common interests of working-class peoples. Representatives from the public schools, the NAACP, the Urban League, and other groups, for example, formed the Committee on School and Community Tensions, but it accomplished little, as segregation hardened many neighborhoods into what the journalist Peter Binzen called "Whitetown." In the first six months of 1955, Philadelphia experienced 213 racial "incidents," mostly along the border between black North Philadelphia and the white working-class communities surrounding it, an area Binzen labeled the "DMZ." In the immediate postwar years, white racism driven by economic fears combined with employer discrimination and structural changes in the economy to eliminate most African Americans' chances at better homes and decent jobs.[48]

By the early to mid-1950s, many blacks were slipping toward poverty. There was a small, well-educated middle class that took advantage of the city's growing white-collar opportunities, but the average household income in 1950 for working-class African Americans stood at only 59 percent of the white level, and that was with many black women contributing their earnings from domestic service. Many blacks were not even that fortunate: one study estimated that the number of manufacturing jobs in North Philadelphia fell by as many as fifty thousand between 1928 and 1972. All along the streets of North Philadelphia, as the historian John Bauman has pointed out, ice-cream factories, battery makers, warehouses, and breweries boarded up their windows, shutting down for good or moving to the suburbs. Urban renewal also took a disproportionate toll on North Philadelphia, reducing the number of residences from 114,000 to 90,000 and clearing away over 600 small businesses. The unemployment rate in the area reached 37 percent by 1956, and another 42 percent claimed to be working only irregularly. By this point African American families constituted 75 percent of those eligible for public housing, and only 2 percent earned the four thousand dollars a year necessary to buy a modest home.[49]

African Americans were of course aware of these bleak employment prospects, and they turned to the NAACP, the Urban League, and other interracial groups for help. As early as November 1944 the NAACP's Spaulding had warned, "The right of Negroes and other minorities to hold jobs in the postwar period [is] of prime importance." Then, in 1946, the organization hired Charles Shorter as executive secretary on the strength of his ten years of experience as an industrial assistant for the Urban League and as a personnel director at Sun Ship. Under Shorter, the NAACP worked with like-minded organizations to get jobs at the Philadelphia Gas Works, the Delaware River Port Authority, and a number of city department stores. Of all the campaigns, the one for department store jobs is the most revealing because it occurred where capital, white workers, paying customers, and black interests all met at one point in a public space.[50]

In their approach to the department stores, black activists turned to the FEPC's strategy of holding quiet meetings and exerting subtle pressure. Although many African Americans found it grating that they could shop in these stores but not work in them, blacks discarded the mass-action approach that had worked so well at the PTC. In part they did this because the NAACP was wracked in these years by charges of "Communist influence" that nearly destroyed the organization, and many were afraid that too much militancy would reopen these issues. Shorter, moreover, was a quieter leader than Moore and felt more comfortable with backroom negotiations. Rather than picket lines and mass marches, the NAACP joined with the Society of Friends and the Council for Equal Job Opportunity to create the Fair Employment Practices in Department Stores committee. Committee members conducted interviews with store managers and tried to persuade them to change their policies. They also asked Philadelphians to write letters or to stop in and ask store owners to rethink their practices.[51]

When African Americans approached store managers, they found men and women who claimed to oppose discrimination but who nonetheless had abundant excuses for not hiring blacks. The fair employment committee first sent Mosetta Freeman, a "well groomed, nicely dressed, brown-skinned girl," to half a dozen downtown stores, including Gimbel's and Lit Brothers, to apply for jobs. All the personnel departments accepted her application, but none offered her employment, even though Blum's had just hired several white women in line in front of Freeman. She asked all of the managers if they followed fair employment practices, and they claimed to do so, but Freeman doubted it. In follow-up interviews, committee members heard one manager after another swear that they hated intolerance (one man called it "damn foolery") but that desegregation could not be pushed; instead it had to "be brought about by education." The personnel manager at Wanamaker's made the point most clearly. "She thought," wrote a fair employment committee member, "that in time [blacks] would be accepted . . . but not in the near future. She thought such a change, however, must not be rushed or come about under pressure." In her opinion, only the education of whites and blacks could change employment patterns and that would not happen in her lifetime. In truth, store managers could have hired African Americans at any time, but, as the Wanamaker's official admitted, the members of the Market Street Store Managers Association had made a pact not to hire blacks as sales clerks. Discrimination was wrong at some rhetorical level, but with their agreement the managers codified Jim Crow as a citywide department store policy. Management's behavior, much like at the PTC, may not have created white working-class racism, but it certainly created a welcoming atmosphere for it.[52]

Managers, after having created a discriminatory environment, followed circular logic to argue that they could not hire blacks because white workers would reject them. One manager said he feared his employees would go out on strike if he hired African Americans. His fears were not unfounded: a couple of years later, white workers at Woolworth's forced management to get rid of newly hired black women or face a walkout. In addition, Gimbel's management transferred a "very efficient and personable Chinese girl" because whites refused to work with her. Rather than standing up for good workers, management fired minorities and defended white jobs, which exacerbated racism in the workplace.[53]

Management's final argument against hiring African Americans was that black sales clerks would drive away white customers. Managers thought whites accepted blacks stocking shelves but would be uncomfortable asking for help from black sales associates, who would appear closer to their level. One manager told Shorter that a store had received seventeen letters of protest when a stock clerk had stepped in to help with selling and intimated that stores would risk their profits by hiring blacks. Committee members conducted interviews with white customers in front of the department stores and found some support for management's view. Responses opposed to black employment ranged from one woman who claimed, "I'm not intolerant, but that's going too far" to people who said, "No, it's not fair to the white sales-girl" or, even more pointedly, "No, send them back South." In these responses whites revealed a fear of losing employment opportunities to black competitors, but it is also important to note that these jobs overwhelmingly went to white women who would then come into more contact with African Americans. One woman, with her daughter in tow, tied the integration of department stores to other realms of life that were equally off-limits in her view. After registering her disapproval of black employees at the store, she told the interviewer she had pulled her daughter out of a school because it accepted black students. She added that she was considering putting her child in a Friends' school, until the interviewer told her that the Friends had desegregated too. "Well!" she said. "I guess we could find an Episcopalian school!"[54]

Respondents with more favorable views seldom spoke in terms of fairness and equality. Instead they drew on their experience of seeing blacks as service workers. Occasionally people said, "Yes, we're Northerners, that's the way we feel about it." But most claimed they would support blacks on the job if it meant quicker service. Some even patronizingly asked why not? "They wait on us for everything else." In all, the surveyors found 60 percent of respondents would accept black employees, but when the fair employment committee broke down its statistics, it found that people's answers depended on the race of the interviewer. Only 42 percent of respondents told white interviewers they agreed with desegregation (percentages for white male and female interviewers were nearly identical). Meanwhile, the black female interviewer got "yes" answers 75 percent of the time, and the black male interviewer heard "yes" 90 percent of the time. This disparity suggests that white Philadelphians recognized the unfairness of their views and sometimes withheld them when talking to African Americans. But when white patrons were in the company of other whites they felt more comfortable expressing their true thoughts. Equal black employment to most of them was unacceptable, and most of those who approved did so only because African Americans would be waiting on them.[55]

After a year of pressure from Philadelphia's black and interracial groups, the department stores gave in. Gimbel's was the first to hire black sales associates, and other stores followed suit. Many did so because Jewish owners, such as Albert Greenfield, felt a certain sympathy for the plight of African Americans, while others recognized that blacks were a growing presence in the city and thus a source of higher revenues. As one historian put it, "Hiring some black workers in public positions was good public relations." Even though blacks won a few jobs in the city's downtown department stores, their gains were tokens that could not reverse the loss of thousands of jobs in the manufacturing sector. Even more, the department store campaign showed just how intractable the employment problem was, as white managers, workers, and customers reinforced a system of white workplace privilege that gave up jobs only grudgingly and in small numbers.[56]

By the early 1950s, black Philadelphians could point to a few gains in the job and housing markets: a handful of positions in formerly all-white sectors, such as retail sales, more homes in some of the white inner suburbs, a foothold in Levittown. But these gains did not offset the bleak picture of a faltering manufacturing base, employers moving to the suburbs and the South, and the use of covenants, discriminatory loans, and violence to create a white suburban ring around the city. Some scholars have pointed to the early 1950s as a "golden age" in black America, with good jobs still available and families intact, but the Philadelphia experience calls this view into question. With the segregation of housing and work, the identification of public housing as inner-city "black" housing, and the growth of black poverty, the early 1950s witnessed the birth of many trends that brought about the later "urban crisis." Many unemployed residents of the Allen Homes probably would have said in the 1950s that the crisis had already begun. Blacks and interracial groups, the Democratic and Republican parties, and white businessmen and workers had to decide how to respond to these problems in subsequent years, and the FEPC emerged as the central issue for all of them. In the politics of the FEPC, the racial lines that had been forming for two decades became abundantly clear.[57]

The Politics of the FEPC

The principle for which [the FEPC] stands is the very bedrock of democracy. How men feel, think and vote on FEPC legislation, therefore, is the true measuring rod of their attitude on the fundamental principle of equality of opportunity for all men.
—*Philadelphia Tribune*, December 1945

On a cold evening in February 1948, seven hundred black and white Philadelphians turned out for a city council meeting. They packed the council chamber's galleries to witness a debate on the hottest political topic in the city: the proposed creation of a Fair Employment Practices Committee (FEPC). Proponents of the organization cast their arguments in the rhetoric of equality and fairness. Richardson Dilworth, the Democratic leader who had just lost a race for mayor, told the council and the crowd that the FEPC was "only a beginning in a campaign for tolerance." Reverend E. Luther Cunningham, who had fought discrimination at the PTC and was a leader in the NAACP, then argued that the committee could address the "Fascist discrimination" plaguing Philadelphia. Most of the crowd cheered the speeches of these two men and a dozen others who took the floor on behalf of the fair employment organization.[1]

The vocal support for an FEPC did not drown out the opposition, who argued that the organization meant nothing more than creeping socialism and government intervention into private affairs. The FEPC ordinance, one man claimed, would help "the Communist movement and Communist infiltration into business and industry." Catherine Brown, head of the far right-wing National Blue Star Mothers, added that the FEPC represented "an act of real revolution" that would destroy the nation, and she "prayed for protection from the many infidels I see here." Seldom did the opponents mention race as a motivating factor, but it was always the subtext. White Philadelphians remembered how the Roosevelt administration's FEPC had helped desegregate the PTC a few years earlier, and they knew that the organization would work to enhance black access to jobs. Kern Dodge, Philadelphia's former director of public safety and a Republican, came closest in this meeting to making explicit the connections between the FEPC, African Americans, and the Democratic Party. After complaining that the government wanted to regulate every aspect of daily life, he told the crowd that the FEPC was just a "cheap political bid for a minority vote." Many in the crowd booed Dodge, but in the back of the room an old man waved an American flag to show his support.[2]

This city council meeting offers a snapshot of a decadelong campaign to secure passage of fair employment legislation at the city and state levels. Throughout the campaign, African Americans put great stock in what they believed the FEPC could accomplish. In their view, the committee would provide equal access to work, but it would also make a statement about the nation's democratic principles. Creation of the committee was, in the words of the *Philadelphia Tribune*, "a great moral issue," a proclamation that the government supported "the proposition that all of its citizens would have the same opportunity to enjoy the fruits of their labor according to their respective abilities." The issue was important enough that many black leaders wanted to make a candidate's stance on the FEPC a litmus test for getting black votes. Democratic leaders, particularly in the reform wing headed by Dilworth and Clark, understood the importance of the black vote to their party and supported the FEPC wholeheartedly. "I strongly favor . . . legislation for a State Fair Employment Practice Commission," Dilworth said in the midst of a campaign for governor. "Living democracy depends upon full civil rights for all of our people."[3]

Republicans had to decide whether they too would back the FEPC. A handful of more liberal leaders in the party supported the committee, which showed that GOP membership did not equate to racist politics. Most, however, opposed it. Their opposition was often quiet, killing legislation in closed committee sessions, voting against the FEPC in secret ballots, and making backroom deals with Joseph Pew, Joseph Grundy, and other wealthy businessmen. In debates, these politicians spoke in euphemisms about "freedom of association," "government intervention," and "socialism" rather than openly attack the FEPC as an instrument of black advancement. Someone listening to their arguments in a vacuum would have had a hard time figuring out whom the FEPC would benefit, but in Philadelphia everyone knew the committee would help African Americans. That is what made the racism of the urban North so hard to combat: at times it hid in plain sight. An examination of the FEPC campaign highlights this racism. George Wallace's strong showing in Milwaukee in 1968, the 1966 civil rights march through Cicero, Illinois, and similar events exposed white vitriol in the 1960s, but the GOP's obstruction of the FEPC twenty years earlier was at least as damaging to African Americans. Republican politicians delayed for a decade the kind of policy African Americans thought they had fought World War II to achieve, and they did so at a time when dwindling employment opportunities made a mockery of the postwar dream for many black Philadelphians. In taking up this fight, Republicans not only prevented passage of the FEPC for years; they also further cemented a cross-class coalition that supplanted interracial liberalism in the city.[4]

The Federal FEPC

The Fair Employment Practices Committee had a particular appeal in Philadelphia because of the 1944 transit strike. People saw how a government order backed with military muscle had swept away decades of discrimination at the PTC, and just a few months after the strike ended black Philadelphians began drawing up plans to support the establishment of permanent federal, state, and city committees. The NAACP led the charge with Carolyn Davenport Moore serving as a lead organizer. In that role she drafted support from the Society of Friends' Committee on Race Relations, the Council for Equal Job Opportunity, and other interracial groups. These organizations believed that a strong FEPC could play a "fundamental part [in] changing the thinking of America" because the committee would make fair employment a government obligation.[5]

Their hopes for a permanent federal agency died in 1946. Ever since the committee's creation in 1941, congressional conservatives had tried to restrict the organization's power by challenging its legitimacy and limiting its appropriations. President Roosevelt had proven to be a lukewarm ally of the committee during the war, especially whenever he thought it interfered with the war effort. But despite this past, in October 1944 (just two months after the PTC strike and a couple of weeks before the election) the president called for "permanent [FEPC] legislation applicable not only to the war emergency but to the peace as well." In his eyes, such legislation fit with previous attempts to outlaw discrimination in New Deal programs. African Americans' service in the war, moreover, meant that, in the words of the president, they deserved "the same opportunity for jobs as other veterans." It was time, Roosevelt concluded, to express the ideal of racial equality "not only as a creed but in a law where [it] can be enforced also in action." Some of this rhetoric was undoubtedly designed to solidify the black vote, but it nonetheless showed where he stood on the issue.[6]

If Roosevelt had lived, he might have been able to force a permanent FEPC through Congress as part of his larger economic bill of rights. It would have been a long shot, as conservatives were gathering strength by the end of the war, but with FDR's death, the chances for a permanent FEPC grew dim. Still, the Philadelphia NAACP pressured the state's elected officials, writing letters to Pennsylvania's eighteen Republican congressmen demanding that they sign a discharge petition to bring a permanent FEPC bill to the floor. The state's fifteen Democratic congressmen, the organization noted, had all signed the petition already. The branch also wrote to President Truman and Republican congressional leaders, saying, "Philadelphia citizens expect [you] to continue [your] fight for an FEPC." But association leaders knew they were waging a losing battle when Congress slashed the FEPC's appropriations and the committee closed its Philadelphia office along with a half dozen others in December 1945. Despite this ominous sign, the *Philadelphia Tribune* continued to press Truman, arguing that the budget cuts had left the FEPC "a shallow mockery . . . of its one-time greatness" and that it would be better to abolish the committee than to let it simply limp along. That way, the editors concluded, "The nation would be honestly proclaiming that it does not intend to effectively fight discrimination."[7]

President Truman ignored the pleas. In his 30,000-word message to Congress in January 1946 he devoted only fourteen words to the FEPC. He may have noted polls showing the country evenly split on the issue (44 percent opposed and 43 percent favored the FEPC) and decided that the political risk was too great. Whatever the reason for Truman's reticence, his speech emboldened congressional conservatives who knew they would not face a stiff fight from Democratic liberals or the White House. The GOP and southern Democrats subsequently filibustered the FEPC to death in early 1946, and by June the organization had gone out of business. These developments made Philadelphia's black rights activists turn to the city and state as arenas for pressing fair employment laws.[8]

As black Philadelphians looked closer to home for fair employment legislation, they saw the Republican Party as their principal foe. By opposing the FEPC and other civil rights measures, the *Tribune* argued in several articles, national Republican leaders had made "a direct and deliberate effort to woo the States Rights Democrats of the South." These politicians knew, the *Tribune* said, that they would have to trade northern black votes for gains in the South, and they were willing to strike that bargain. The paper concluded that such a move ran counter to everything the Republican Party had represented for nearly a century, and it warned the GOP that it dare not "swallow the solid south," for doing so would betray African Americans and bring "dishonor upon the saintly Abraham Lincoln."[9]

The *Tribune*'s analysis of trends in Republican racial politics well described much of the GOP's behavior across the country. At the national level, progressive business leaders charged Ohio senator Robert Taft with "double-dealing" for his backroom opposition to the FEPC. Republican congressmen and senators appeared at a party rally in Washington, D.C., where ten thousand supporters waved rebel flags and shouted "No!" whenever speakers asked if they wanted an FEPC. And the Republican Party, drawing on long-standing southern rhetoric, dropped an FEPC pledge from its 1952 platform, claiming it was "the primary responsibility of each State to order and control its own domestic institutions." At the state level, Republican legislators across the country opposed the creation of local FEPCs. Some claimed they would cost too much money while others took up the argument of New York's GOP that fair employment organizations would "incite racial tension." Pennsylvania's Republican members of the House of Representatives refused to sign discharge petitions and even led the effort to dilute the proposed permanent federal FEPC. Representative Samuel McConnell of Montgomery County offered a bill that added discrimination based on political affiliation, sex, and physical disabilities to the provisions outlawing racial and religious discrimination. His proposal also eliminated any enforcement powers for the agency and declared that the absence of individuals of a particular race, religion, or nationality was not evidence of discrimination. McConnell's bill won approval from nine of Pennsylvania's eighteen Republican representatives, but not one of the state's fifteen Democrats supported it: they found the bill too weak, and no one lamented when conservatives killed it shortly thereafter. Democratic leaders, in a thinly veiled attack on the Republicans, told the black press they wanted an FEPC with "teeth in it" because the "anti-semiti[sm], race hatred and bigotry that we have in our country today must go." Given this background, black leaders in Philadelphia turned to the Democrats to help pass a city FEPC that they knew the Republicans would oppose.[10]

The City FEPC and Local Politics

Local black leaders cast the debate over passage of the city FEPC in moral terms. African Americans, the NAACP argued, had given their lives in World War II, and America could no longer justify denying a man "an opportunity to hold a job according to his ability;—just because God made him brown or black instead of white." Bayard Rustin supported this view, telling a Philadelphia audience that "negative attitudes toward minority groups have come as a direct result of segregation" and that the FEPC was a vital means of "changing such attitudes." Ordinary African Americans heard these arguments and many more in the pages of the *Philadelphia Tribune* and got involved, holding mass meetings, writing thousands of letters to elected officials, and attending church services that urged passage of fair employment legislation. Within a year of V-J Day, there was a groundswell of black support for a local FEPC.[11]

Support came from outside the black community as well. Jewish groups, knowing discrimination affected them too, backed the proposed agency strongly. Jewish Community Relations Council officials appeared on radio programs with the NAACP to discuss how the FEPC could benefit all minorities, and Jewish Democrats drafted the first city FEPC bill. Catholic organizations also joined the cause, which showed there was no easy dividing line with liberal Jews on one side and racist Catholics on the other. Instead, each community had members who supported black rights and members who opposed them. Irish Catholics, for example, formed a chapter of the Catholic Interracial Council to push for an FEPC that would "cleanse the nation of an anti-democratic and anti-Christian hypocrisy." Catholics also served as the first leaders of the city FEPC once it was created. The Society of Friends, the Council for Equal Job Opportunity, and other organizations gave their support as well. A combination of religious conviction, CIO-style commitment to interracial workplace solidarity, and belief in the liberal alliance forged a decade earlier in the New Deal seemed to fire these white supporters of the FEPC. As they joined with African Americans to champion a fair employment committee for the city, it was obvious that liberal politics still had some potency.[12]

Democratic leaders recognized this progressive alliance gathering around the FEPC and helped guide it. Dilworth and Clark in particular pushed the agency as a means of reconfiguring race relations in the city. Like many liberal politicians in the postwar years, Dilworth at times placed equal rights in the context of the Cold War. How, he asked, could the United States preach "the standards of tolerance to the entire world" if it refused to establish fair employment practices? This failure, he continued, "can be used by Communists everywhere as a real propaganda setback to democratic forces." He then charged the Republicans with undermining the FEPC and warned that he and his party would use it as a campaign issue in the black community at every opportunity. Two leading black politicians, Joseph Rainey and Robert Nix, appeared with Dilworth on a number of occasions where they urged voters to support the Democrats because of the party's stance on the FEPC. Some Democratic ward leaders, sensing restlessness among white voters, feared Dilworth was pushing the issue too hard. Most notably in Polish neighborhoods, they vocally sided with their communities in questioning the FEPC's agenda. Polls showed that Clark's views made him unpopular with many white working-class citizens and that only blacks gave him strong support. At Democratic meetings Clark occasionally heard boos and angry murmurs about his progressive policies. Republicans saw the dissension and anonymously commented to the press that Dilworth and Clark "would lose more than [they] would gain by harping on a matter which has aroused controversy wherever it has come up."[13]

Republicans were right in their comments about the dangers the FEPC presented to the Democrats. James Reichley, an astute observer of Philadelphia politics, found a "smouldering hostility toward the Negroes . . . present among all of the city's white groups: Protestants, Jews, Irish, and Italians, as well as Poles." Jews were the least antiblack of all the groups, Reichley argued, with their suburban neighborhoods constituting "a Democratic island among acres of suburban Irish and Italians and Germans who ha[d] drifted into the [Republican] party." Working-class whites were angry because they faced black competition for jobs, and many blamed the Democrats for making matters worse by supporting the FEPC. Rather than the party of "Rum, Romanism, and Rebellion," Reichley wrote, to many whites the Democrats had become the party of "Jews, Socialism, and Negroes." Such antiblack feelings were "the most potentially dynamic factor in Philadelphia politics" and could "blow the Democratic coalition sky high."[14]

As Democratic leaders supported black workplace rights and many white Philadelphians blanched at the move, Republicans portrayed themselves as the defenders of white prerogatives in the city FEPC campaign. That campaign came to a head in a series of city council meetings in February 1948. The press and black organizations knew the meetings would be contentious: for three years African Americans had been building toward this date while at the same time city councilmen had started formulating their arguments against the fair employment organization. Members of the all-Republican council argued that change had to come slowly and that a strong FEPC was dangerous because it would "discriminate" against whites. David Jameson, who was the most forceful proponent of this view, argued that he opposed the FEPC because it was "unconstitutional and because if it were passed it would intensify hatred." "When you legislate for one group," he continued, "you legislate against everybody else, because our constitution says— everybody is created equal." Frank O'Connor, another FEPC opponent, took a different tack, arguing that any demands for change were the result of "Communistic agitation." This and other caustic comments led black Philadelphians to picket his home in South Philadelphia and send a delegation to meet with him at his office. There, he made his views on African Americans more obvious, talking about their supposedly criminal natures and then ordering NAACP officials to leave.[15]

These politicians drew much of their rhetoric from the city's business community. Through letters and emissaries to the councilmen's offices, business leaders made their views known. The chamber of commerce argued that "the FEPC agitation is a Communist plot" and had to be defeated. Minorities, the chamber continued, made up less than a quarter of the population, but their concerns received disproportionate attention. Other businesses and organizations, including the Philadelphia Textile Manufacturers Association, Cahall Advertising Company, and Semans & Co., claimed they were "not anti-Negro" in opposing the FEPC but that the government had no right to "interfere" with their hiring practices. Many of these businessmen had a deep-seated aversion to government oversight and seldom used overtly racist arguments, but in opposing the FEPC, they resisted an organization that African Americans widely believed would help them achieve equality. Their campaign, whether motivated by laissez-faire economic views, racism, or most likely a mixture of both, nonetheless amounted to a "silent war," in the Tribune's words, and its editors feared that the offensive would work.[16]

Other groups, such as the National Blue Star Mothers, were more willing to employ openly racist rhetoric. Led by Catherine Brown and Lillian Parks, the organization took the title to confuse people into thinking they were part of the Blue Star Mothers (a support group for women with children in the military). In fact, the National Blue Star Mothers was a right-wing, anti-Semitic, racist organization with ties to the equally racist and anti-Semitic minister Gerald L. K. Smith and the Ku Klux Klan. During World War II the group had attacked the president as "Jew Roosevelt" and posted handbills charging that the "Jew war" was an attempt to create one world government for "Jew international bankers." Organization leaders also applauded the PTC strike, writing that the "people of Philadelphia had guts enough to riot at the PTC hiring Jews and Niggers. I wish we had held out longer." They also sent letters to Governor Martin, urging him to institute racial segregation in Philadelphia. After the war, the organization worked with a right-wing publisher in Frankford who wanted to ban immigration by Asians, Africans, and non-Christians. Only by preserving the racial and religious purity of the United States, the group believed, could Americans "preserve [their] Republic, Constitution, and Freedom." Battling the FEPC was just an extension of the politics the National Blue Star Mothers had been practicing for a decade.[17]

In their attacks, the organization's leaders hit all the right chords, blasting the FEPC as a communistic, unconstitutional, Jewish-inspired threat to the previously "harmonious" relationship between whites and blacks. "Do you know," asked one National Blue Star Mothers poster, "that this proposed legislation is the brainchild of the followers of Karl Marx? That the strategy for effecting passage of this legislation . . . was planned, in part, by the American Jewish Congress?" This bill, the poster asserted, had "nothing whatever to do with fairness, employment, or good practice." Instead, it was designed to create a "gestapo" that would rob employers of their rights and abolish "all constitutional guarantees provided by the Bill of Rights." Even worse, the group contended, was the fact that everything had been fine between the races until a small group of agitators had stirred up trouble. "Before this small noisy minority arrived on the scene Americans were not conscious of such words as 'race, creed, color,'" wrote the group. "There was no such thing as 'classes.' Everybody was American, conscious only of the fact that the Bill of Rights provided all that was necessary for their protection."[18]

The arguments used by leaders of the National Blue Star Mothers attempted to turn the liberal case for an FEPC on its head. Opposition to a fair employment agency, they claimed, was the patriotic position. People who wanted the FEPC were not trying to make America live up to its creed but were in fact trying to subvert what the nation stood for. With a government agency supervising hiring practices, employers would lose their centuries-old rights, Communists would gain further entry into American society, and previously placid race relations would grow stormy. Only defeating the FEPC could prevent this supposed fate. Such views aligned the National Blue Star Mothers with the Republican Party. Liberals, then, did not just have to make their case for fair employment to a skeptical white public; they also had to counter the arguments of organized racist opponents who were working in tandem with the city's business community and long-dominant GOP.

When the city council convened on February 19, 1948, its members were caught between two vocal campaigns pulling on the FEPC from opposite directions. Councilmen had heard from the National Blue Star Mothers and the business community but had also received many letters, petitions, and personal visits from FEPC supporters over the last couple of months, and they saw that the galleries were full that night. The council, comprised of twenty-two Republicans and no Democrats, understood that open opposition would inflame the audience, so council members pulled back from their strongest rhetoric. Instead of immediately scuttling the organization, they gave the floor to Richardson Dilworth, E. Luther Cunningham, and a dozen other

FEPC proponents who made the case for fair employment. National Blue Star Mothers leaders and a few others were there to protest, but their voices were overmatched by the crowd.[19]

The council, led by Wallace Egan, who represented Irish West Philadelphia, wanted no part of the FEPC but could not admit that publicly, so members privately constructed a compromise that crippled the proposed committee with amendments. One clause stated that hiring would still be based on the "character, merit, experience and ability" of applicants. Employers could of course define those qualities however they saw fit, which opened a loophole for many to get around hiring African Americans. Another amendment held that the FEPC could only open an investigation if someone filed charges, and it allowed complainants only sixty days to make a claim. This placed the entire burden on African Americans to identify discriminatory employers, figure out how to use the FEPC apparatus, and do so within two months of being denied a job or promotion. Even if a black worker properly followed all of these steps, another Egan amendment allowed employers to appeal FEPC findings to a city commission. Not only would businessmen find a more agreeable audience for their appeal on the commission, the statute again placed the onus on individual African Americans to continue pressing their claims. Finally, the FEPC had few enforcement powers after the council finished with it: it could only fine an employer up to one hundred dollars. Egan's finishing stroke was to include every city employer, down to those with just one employee, under the FEPC's purview. The original legislation had exempted businesses with fewer than fifteen employees to assure small firms they could hire family members without interference. Egan designed this amendment, the *Tribune* charged, to "be on the record in favor of FEPC in the face of unprecedented support from minority groups" while at the same time trying to "defeat the bill by includ[ing] an unworkable provision." Several FEPC proponents agreed with the newspaper's assessment, telling reporters that Egan and the rest of the council were "muddying the waters" with all of these amendments in an attempt to eviscerate the bill. At the end of the discussion, the city council approved Egan's amendments and then tabled the legislation for future consideration. African Americans left the meeting disgruntled that they still had no FEPC and that the proposed committee had so many limitations.[20]

After pigeonholing the legislation for three weeks, the council agreed to put it to a vote. Nineteen of twenty-two councilmen voted for the FEPC. Of the other three, two were absent because of business or illness, and Frank O'Connor, who had spoken of blacks as criminals and thrown NAACP representatives out of his office, refused to attend the meeting. The FEPC had finally passed, and the *Tribune* rejoiced that the city council had placed the government behind legislation that permitted a man to "do the kind of work for which he is best fitted regardless of race, creed or color."[21]

Such joy was premature, the *Tribune*'s editors discovered, as Egan's amendments and the council's true feelings soon hobbled the organization. The city council first stymied the FEPC by withholding its funding, granting no money to the organization for eight months. When the funding finally came through, commissioners found they had only $67,000, and three-quarters of that was designated for use in 1949. All told, 80 percent of the FEPC's budget went to paying salaries, which left little money for operating expenses, publicity in the black community, and other necessary activities. New York City's FEPC, by contrast, received $370,000 to carry out its mission. Even this parsimonious funding was too much for some Philadelphians who complained to the press about so much money going to an "un-American" organization. The situation was so bad that the *Pittsburgh Courier*, surveying the council's behavior and the reaction of the public, feared that the FEPC had been created merely out of "political expedience" and represented insincerity at its worst.[22]

Limited by scant resources and the Egan amendments, FEPC members relied on educational programs to push for black employment rights. Their go-slow, nonconfrontational approach, while representative of much of the interracialist thinking of the day, excluded more aggressive tactics. The idea of the FEPC launching investigations, suing defiant employers, and helping ordinary people engage in grassroots activism was off the table. Instead, the committee gave hundreds of talks to businesses and civic organizations; distributed literature through the mail, movie theaters, and political parties; held fair employment weeks; and gave out stickers that read, "Americans Ask: Is He a Good Worker? Not What Is His Race or Religion? Support Fair Employment Practices." Committee members, unable to think beyond their educational program—or perhaps tacitly acknowledging that they could do little else—assured the public that their campaign was working. "We look upon our educational program as the key to continued progress in promoting employment on merit," they wrote. "Prejudice and . . . untested fears tend to evaporate when people work together and get to know each other better." Those statements were true to an extent, but as black employment rates fell in the early 1950s, the committee's focus on education looked increasingly inadequate. In six years the organization fielded some twelve thousand complaints but investigated only 10 percent of them. In only four hundred cases did the committee find discrimination taking place, and it never once used its limited enforcement powers to hold public hearings or to fine or press charges against an employer. The local FEPC, as the city council intended, was a watchdog with no teeth.[23]

Still, black Philadelphians were generally positive about the organization. They clearly understood its shortcomings, but black observers believed that the mere existence of the city FEPC made an important statement about their rights as citizens. The organization embodied a "great democratic principle," in the words of the *Tribune*, because "Democracy is not just majority rule, but majority rule with respect for the rights of minorities." On a more practical level, Theodore Spaulding and other local black leaders saw the city FEPC as both a limited replacement for the defunct national FEPC and a stepping-stone toward a state organization. These leaders knew what was happening in Philadelphia—the suburbanization of housing and jobs accompanied by discriminatory policies that kept blacks out of northeast Philadelphia and the surrounding counties—and they knew that even a strong local FEPC could not touch problems outside the city's boundaries. The solution, NAACP leader Milo Manly asserted, was a state commission designed to handle racial discrimination on a broader basis. The Commission on Human Relations (COHR) and other organizations agreed with Manly that the metropolitan area had exceeded the "frozen political boundaries" of the city and that "the existing governmental structure of the metropolitan area is failing to meet the needs of the larger community." The state, in COHR's view, had to pass legislation that brought the suburban counties under the control of a stronger FEPC modeled on Philadelphia's organization. Aware of the bittersweet results of their city campaign, Philadelphia's African Americans and their white liberal allies set out to pass a state FEPC.[24]

The State FEPC and Pennsylvania Politics

The state campaign, even more than that in the city, highlighted the way business leaders, the Republican Party, and many ordinary white Pennsylvanians came together to oppose black equality. In the city, businessmen and their Republican allies had smeared the FEPC as "Communistic," "un-American," and a Democratic grab for minority votes. Those tactics had found much support and had given the city council the nod to cripple the organization. Still, blacks constituted a large enough part of Philadelphia's population that the council had found it prudent to pass an FEPC, albeit a weak one, rather than incite such a large group of voters. But outside of Philadelphia, African Americans formed only a small portion of the state's population, and politicians had to pay far less attention to their concerns. Even more, the state's biggest businessmen, Joseph Pew of Sun Oil and Joseph Grundy and G. Mason Owlett of the Pennsylvania Manufacturers' Association (PMA), had only limited holdings in Philadelphia, but they opposed any "interference" with their business practices in the state. When FEPC proponents turned to the state legislature, they faced a stronger, more sustained counterattack than anything the Philadelphia Chamber of Commerce could muster. Republican legislators from northeast Philadelphia and Montgomery and Bucks counties, with help from rural counties across the state, worked closely with big business to oppose the FEPC. These Republican politicians with close ties to the state's biggest businessmen received significant support from newly suburbanized working-class white Philadelphians, a sign that the GOP's cross-class alliance was coming to fruition.

FEPC advocates argued that African Americans had to pressure the state's politicians, particularly those in the Republican Party, to get the organization established. The FEPC was, in the NAACP's terms, a "measuring rod for all political candidates," and black voters needed to know a person's stance on fair employment legislation before deciding how to vote. Although officially nonpartisan, NAACP leaders quietly commented, "While we must keep after the Democrats, it is really the Republicans we must work on." The GOP, Moore noted, had tied up the initial FEPC bill in committee, and a discharge petition had failed, by a count of 102–97, to bring the legislation to the floor. Only four Republicans voted in favor of the FEPC, whereas every Democrat supported the organization. The bill's initial failure in April 1945, in Moore's view, fell squarely on the Republicans' shoulders, and in speeches and bulletins she let her constituents know it. In fact, her rhetoric grew so partisan that national officer Ella Baker cautioned the local NAACP to rein her in. Baker was concerned that blaming the Republicans "might be interpreted as pro-democratic or anti-republican sentiment." It was better, she believed, to "simply stat[e] the record without comment" and let the public draw its own conclusions.[25]

In admonishing local leaders to avoid partisan politics, Baker displayed the NAACP's continuing faith in working with both parties to promote black rights, but subsequent Republican behavior showed how little interest the GOP had in working with African Americans. One delegation went to Governor Martin's office only to be denied an audience: he claimed he was too busy with state business. Martin may indeed have been busy, but his failure to act during the transit strike had already made many African Americans suspicious of his views, and a 1946 campaign flier confirmed their beliefs. In that anonymous circular, Martin supporters told whites in North Philadelphia that voting Republican would "Keep the N . . . in His Place." "If you want our Capitol to look like Uncle Tom's cabin VOTE DEMOCRATIC," the flier continued. "Elect Rice [the Democratic gubernatorial candidate] for Governor— the N . . . Lover. . . . The next session of the Legislature the Democrats will pass the N . . . . F.E.P.C. Bill. . . . Martin has kept the N . . . . in his place. . . . COME OUT AND VOTE THE STRAIGHT REPUBLICAN TICKET AND KEEP PENNSYLVANIA WHITE." In that flier, Martin, or at least his supporters, tied blacks and the Democratic Party together and made it clear that the only way to stop black advancement and the FEPC was by electing Republican candidates. In that election cycle, Martin left the governor's office to run for the U.S. Senate. He defeated the New Dealer Joseph Guffey by six hundred thousand votes (twenty percentage points) statewide, receiving his greatest pluralities in Philadelphia in the white districts of the city's far north. Suburban counties gave him 73 percent of their vote. Martin's only sharp setbacks in the area came in some black districts in North and West Philadelphia, but those votes were a drop in the bucket compared to the support the state gave him. Other Republican politicians showed less open racism, but they too made it clear that they would not support the FEPC. Rep. Robert Rich, for example, argued that the FEPC would actually harm African Americans. The FEPC, he said, was "only an illusion by some people to still further the interest of *communism* in this country." "I am not against the colored people and have always been an admirer of . . . Booker T. Washington," he continued. "Now I believe if he were here today that he would agree that the FEPC is only a smoke screen," one that "would do them great harm and make them less self reliant."[26]

Other Republicans went beyond Rich's sophistry and turned to threats. John Grantham, a black Baptist leader in Norristown in suburban Montgomery County, described his arch-Republican community for the national NAACP. The county, one of the richest in the nation, had a long history of Republican dominance that Franklin Roosevelt had scarcely touched. Even in his landslide victory in 1936, the president lost the county by eight thousand votes, and in 1948 and again in 1952 the Democrats lost there by over forty thousand ballots. Republicans ruled Montgomery County, and they kept, as Grantham put it, a "stranglehold" on the area's blacks. In part they maintained their dominance by holding preelection rallies where ordinary African Americans got the chance to shake hands with state politicians. Local Republican leaders also gave menial jobs to blacks in the county courthouse and dispensed patronage to black leaders. The unspoken condition for these "favors" was that African Americans had to vote Republican and could not challenge the status quo. Republican leaders from the county, including Lt. Gov. Lloyd Wood and several members of the PMA, made it clear that they gave jobs and patronage and that they could take both away. Local blacks, Grantham stated, knew they were being closely watched and that their jobs would disappear if they failed to "walk in step with the political set-up." Few things angered local Republicans more than talk of the FEPC, and when Wood ran for governor in 1954 he refused even to address fair employment as a campaign issue. In Montgomery County, no blacks dared bring up the FEPC at political rallies. African Americans were so cowed, Grantham concluded, that they could "not make any progress in this town as long as the Negro voter is afraid to assert his rights as a citizen who demands to be heard."[27]

With Montgomery County's politics a representative, if extreme, version of many of Philadelphia's suburbs, FEPC bills faced serious opposition in the state legislature from the start. Democratic representative Homer Brown, a black attorney from Pittsburgh and a member of the NAACP's national board of directors, introduced the first state FEPC bill in 1945. His proposal, which became a model for all future legislation, had four features: it established an independent, salaried commission; it gave the FEPC the power to investigate complaints, issue cease-and-desist orders, and take matters to the courts where statute violators would face fines and jail time; it declared discrimination by race, color, creed, national origin, or ancestry unlawful; and it brought employers, government agencies, and unions under the FEPC's purview. For two months the bill languished in the labor committee, registering only silence from the governor's mansion and the offices of the Republican leadership. Finally, in April 1945, Brown told the press that Martin's "refusal to give any statement in favor of the bill, so far as I can ascertain, shows he is against it." "Hidden forces," Brown continued, reside "in high places in our State Government" and are "spreading the poison of racial hatred and religious bigotry." Those "hidden forces," according to the *Tribune*, included Governor Martin and the state chamber of commerce.[28]

Governor Martin took the lead in opposing the FEPC. He often claimed to believe in "complete tolerance and equal opportunities and rights for all," but this belief never translated into action on behalf of black Pennsylvanians. He rejected the FEPC, claiming that its projected budget of a half-million dollars a year would cost too much. He also asserted on a number of occasions that the organization would fail because only education could change people's thoughts and behaviors. All the state's money, he said, would go to waste if the fair employment law had "criminal features," because such compulsion would only lead to angry reactions. These views had certain affinities with southern segregationists, who often claimed they had nothing against African Americans per se but that the government had no right to tell white citizens whom to hire or associate with. Such arguments had little validity to African Americans, who during the transit strike, had seen what state power could do to curb discrimination. By 1946, the governor's antiblack stance had become so obvious that he was "persona non grata with the majority of Negroes," in the *Tribune*'s words.[29]

Martin's views came in part from an honest philosophical commitment to smaller government and in part from an unwillingness to advance black equality. Throughout his political career, he argued that "a government which gives the people everything they want will soon take everything they have." The editors of Philadelphia's suburban newspapers echoed such sentiments, consistently carrying articles denouncing "government power" and "coercion." Everything from "socialized medicine" to progressive taxation to "senseless Government opposition to large and small business" was open to attack. The mistrust of state power showed by Martin and those who shared his political views, then, was not just about race. But often, especially in the case of the FEPC, government power and black advancement were intertwined. In his mail, Martin received many letters opposed to the FEPC. As a politician with aspirations for the U.S. Senate if not the presidency, he knew he had to listen to the state's white voters, and they told him over and over that he, in the words of one constituent, had to stop the "Fair Employment Practices Act," which was the "very sick child of the New Deal Democrats." If the law passed, Harry Klinefelter continued, "Uncle Sam's agents will be given the right to tell most employers whom they must employ; then it won't be long before these same New Deal agents will be telling practically all employees for whom they must work." In his letter, Klinefelter represented the views of many whites who saw the FEPC as a twin threat to employer prerogatives and white jobs. Many whites, employers and workers, had come to believe they had more to fear from blacks, the FEPC, and the government than from each other. The FEPC, in this view, was part of a broader government agenda to reshape American society, and whites believed they had to oppose it or lose their traditional "rights." For Martin and many of his supporters, black gains from an FEPC went hand-in-hand with the extension of the liberal state, and Martin, who frequently denounced the latter as "Un-American," found the two nearly inseparable.[30]

In addition to appeasing many of the state's white voters, Martin's opposition to the FEPC also pleased Pennsylvania's big businessmen, especially Grundy and Owlett of the PMA. This was an important consideration in a state where, one observer noted, "From 1921 until at least the 1950s no one received the Republican gubernatorial nomination unless he had the approval of the leaders" of the PMA. Grundy and Joseph Pew of Sun Oil and Sun Shipbuilding had supported Martin in his 1942 bid for the governorship and, according to the *Pittsburgh Courier*, made it clear that they would not back him for the Senate in 1946 if he endorsed the FEPC. Martin opposed the committee and ended up enjoying his Senate seat for two terms, from 1947 to 1959. The *Tribune* noted that this obvious, heavy-handed manipulation meant that right-wing, reactionary politics was alive and well in the Commonwealth.[31]

Although the *Tribune* tagged this politics "Grundyism," the name applied just as well to a wide array of businessmen in the state. Grundy's right-hand man, G. Mason Owlett, met with state legislators every year from 1945 to 1953 to make sure that FEPC bills failed. Once in 1949, at a time when progressives seemed to be making headway, he emerged from a private meeting with Republican governor James Duff (Martin's successor) and several state legislators to announce that the "Pennsylvania Republican Party was now united" and that passage of the FEPC was "unlikely." He had told the politicians, according to the *Philadelphia Independent*, that "if they expected his support . . . they had better not vote for the FEPC bill." His threat undoubtedly carried extra weight with Governor Duff, who had higher political aspirations, since Owlett was a member of the Republican National Committee. Duff won a U.S. Senate seat a year later. On another occasion, to make it clear where the business community stood on the FEPC, Owlett ripped a copy of an FEPC bill out of the hands of a legislator.[32]

Other corporate leaders used less blatant tactics but opposed the fair employment committee just the same. The Pennsylvania Railroad, Bell Telephone, the state chamber of commerce, Sun Oil, and the Pennsylvania Hotels Association all expressed their disapproval of a fair employment committee. As was often the case, their race-based opposition was veiled. The hotel association, for example, complained that the law would give the government too much power. The chamber of commerce, however, dropped any pretense of subterfuge, bluntly complaining that the state was using "compulsion" to force "harassed employers" into hiring "unqualified" blacks and Jews. Some of the strongest opposition came from Joseph Pew of Sun Oil who had made his views on race obvious during World War II, when he established his segregated shipyard. Pew had moved even further to the right since the war, publicly rejoicing when FDR died that the president's "golden voice now has been stilled" and offering money to churches if they expressed a sufficiently conservative line. Pew and his family later supported the far-right John Birch Society, which, according to the historian Philip Jenkins, had great strength in Philadelphia's white suburbs. In the late 1940s and early 1950s, however, it was enough for Pew to express his politics by, in the *Tribune*'s words, "sneaking up in the dark and sticking a dagger in [the FEPC's] back."[33]

Just as the state's Republican governors listened to the will of many white voters and the business community, so too did lower-ranking politicians. They knew that opposing the FEPC would bring both votes and the gratitude of corporate leaders. Like Governor Martin they particularly decried the FEPC for being coercive. The law, Rep. Robert Rich argued, would "bring about regimentation thus destroying a free and liberty loving nation." Others said the committee was dangerous because it tried to "control a moral issue," to "legislate the brotherhood of man." A clear Republican strategy emerged in the legislature and governor's mansion as politicians continuously argued that the FEPC was a coercive organization that no one really wanted. Coupling that argument with the disdain many whites and the business community held for fair employment legislation made it easy for the GOP to justify stymieing any FEPC bill brought to the legislature.[34]

Year after year Republicans employed the same tactics and thereby became adept at killing FEPC legislation. Rather than holding an open debate on the floor of the legislature, where Democrats could seize the moral high ground, they pigeonholed FEPC bills in the judiciary or labor committees, where they used the secret ballot to prevent fair employment bills from reaching the floor. Although the ballots were secret, observers could always tell which way members had voted on the FEPC: Democrats emerged from sessions to declare their support while Republicans refused to discuss the issue. A few representatives, such as Edward Gallagher from far northeast Philadelphia, would not so cryptically tell the press, "I'm a party line man," but most Republicans remained quiet, confident that the issue would never reach the floor. Exceptions to the party line came only from a handful of Republicans from Philadelphia districts with growing black populations. Senator A. Evans Kephart from South Philadelphia, for example, voted with the Democrats in favor of the FEPC in 1951, but his vote was essentially meaningless because he knew full well that the measure would be shot down by the suburban and rural members of the Judiciary Committee. Then, after the bill was defeated, Kephart, who chaired the committee, told the press he would not consider the legislation again, even though Democrats were agitating for another vote. "Nobody is for it," he told the *Tribune*, ignoring unanimous

Democratic support. This strategy of death by committee became so common that by 1953 Jewish Community Relations Council staff members resignedly told each other that the FEPC had been killed, yet again, "in the usual manner."[35]

Republicans from urban districts in Philadelphia and Pittsburgh were cautious enough about rising black political power that they suggested alternatives to the strict Brown bill and its progeny rather than openly oppose the legislation. They offered a slew of amendments that would have crippled the organization by, among other things, staffing it with unpaid volunteers, giving employers the right to reject applicants who did not "fit into the business," and asking that studies be conducted to "examine" the situation. All this was an attempt, the *Tribune* argued, to "muddy the waters" and distract Pennsylvanians from creating a robust FEPC. Some proponents of the fair employment committee leveled stronger charges: state senator Sam Neff accused the Judiciary Committee of "bias and bigotry," while other Democratic politicians alluded to a certain "friendliness to the KKK" when discussing Republican racial politics. African Americans offered the sharpest rebuke of the Republicans, with one man arguing that the GOP was hurting America in the Cold War. "Peoples in South America, Asia, Africa and Europe," he argued, "are aware of [America's] double face talk of democracy." Only the FEPC, he continued, would allow the United States to implement the "real practice of democracy." The *Philadelphia Tribune* warned the Republicans that their votes on the FEPC damaged the "honor of the Republican party." The FEPC, the paper argued, "supports the great principle of the equality of mankind," and the GOP could not escape its responsibility for repeatedly killing the legislation. Ordinary black voters supported the *Tribune*'s thinking. "The citizenry," warned one woman, "is fast becoming disgruntled and has come to lose much faith in the G.O.P." Governor Martin should give his "full support . . . to any measure seeking [equal employment] rights for Penna Negroes," said another Philadelphian. "If [he] cannot support this program Negroes should know it." Through the politics of the FEPC, it was becoming more and more evident that Republicans and African Americans were parting ways.[36]

As the FEPC became more central to electoral politics and criticism of the GOP mounted, Philadelphia Democrats, led by Richardson Dilworth, pressed fair employment as a campaign issue. Because Dilworth had a long track record of supporting black rights, his calls for fair employment came across not as a political ploy, but as a heartfelt stand for equality. The FEPC, he told the press, would be a "red hot political issue" in every election until the state

delphia Transportation Company 3-BR-246 (Philadelphia, PA), box 343, FFEPC; Ross, *All Manner of Men*, 91; *Philadelphia Tribune*, Dec. 11, 1943, 1; Francis Biddle to Franklin Roosevelt, Jan. 29, 1943, folder Civil Rights/Fair Employment, box Aliens and Immigration—Correspondence: A–H, container 1, Francis Biddle Papers, Hyde Park, N.Y.; James Bristol to A. J. Muste, Aug. 28, 1944, folder Philadelphia Transportation Company Strike, 1944, box 16, FOR.

For a history of America's war effort that laments the "necessitarian" approach that focused entirely on winning the war at the expense of domestic reform, see Blum, *V Was for Victory*.

27. "Statement Filed with the FEPC," Dec. 8, 1943, "Summary of the Evidence with Opinion and Order," Dec. 8, 1943, folder Philadelphia Transportation Company 3-BR-246 (Philadelphia, PA), box 343, FFEPC; Maurice Mersky to G. James Fleming, Nov. 24, 1943, Mary Kuller to U.S. Gov't. Fair Employment Practices Committee, Nov. 23, 1943, folder Newspaper Clipping and Letters from Public PTC Case, box 3, PFEPC.

28. George Crockett to George Johnson, Jan. 15, 1943, talk by Frank Colbourn [*sic*], Dec. 14, 1943, Frank Carney to Malcolm Ross, Jan. 3, 1944, folder Philadelphia Transportation Company 3-BR-246 (Philadelphia, PA), box 343, FFEPC; *Philadelphia Inquirer*, Jan. 6, 1944, 1.

29. Dierenfield, *Keeper of the Rules*; Olson, *Historical Dictionary of the New Deal*, 461–62.

For more on southern contempt for the New Deal, see Sitkoff, *A New Deal for Blacks*; Egerton, *Speak Now against the Day*; Patterson, *Congressional Conservatism*; Katznelson, Geiger, and Kryder, "Limiting Liberalism."

30. *Chicago Defender*, Jan. 22, 1944, 4; clippings from *Philadelphia Afro-American*, Jan. 15, 1944, and unnamed and undated newspaper in Scrapbook of Clippings, 1943–45, box 52, PNAACP; Richard Frankensteen to Howard Smith, Jan. 7, 1944, Office File 4245g, FDRP; *Pittsburgh Courier*, Jan. 15, 1944, 1.

31. U.S. Congress, House Special Committee to Investigate Executive Agencies, *To Investigate the Executive Agencies*, 1874–81; *Chicago Defender*, Jan. 22, 1944, 4.

32. U.S. Congress, House Special Committee to Investigate Executive Agencies, *To Investigate the Executive Agencies*, 1885–1901, 1925–26; *Chicago Defender*, Jan. 22, 1944, 4.

33. Freeman, "Transport Workers Union," 868; U.S. Congress, House Committee on Un-American Activities, *Investigation of Un-American Propaganda Activities in the United States*, 8095, 8112; Freeman, *In Transit*, 354.

34. Freeman, *In Transit*, 151–55; Bracey and Meier, *Papers of the NAACP*, Part 13, Series A, reel 19.

35. Borgnis, *An Inside Story*, 32; clipping in folder Evening Bulletin Transit Collection, Urban Archives; *Transport Workers Bulletin*, Sept. 1943, 10, Apr. 1943, 1, Aug. 1943, 6.

36. *Transport Workers Bulletin*, July 1943, 3; Freeman, "Transport Workers Union," 675–77.

37. *Transport Workers Bulletin*, May 1943, 3, Jan.–Feb. 1944, 1; "United—Invincible,"

Mar. 24, 1943, folder Local 234 (Phil.) Jan.–July 1943, box 81, TWUP; Roberts, "A History and Analysis," 182–84; clipping in folder Clips *Bulletin* Strikes—Transit—1943 Phila., box 227A, MC.

For more on the way rank-and-file racism often constrained CIO leaders, see Nelson, *Divided We Stand*, 185–218; Nelson, "Class, Race, and Democracy in the CIO," 351–74. For a vigorous rebuttal of Nelson's argument, see Faue, "'Anti-Heroes of the Working Class,'" 375–88.

38. Bracey and Meier, *Papers of the NAACP*, Part 13, Series A, reel 19; Meier and Rudwick, "Communist Unions," 186; *Pittsburgh Courier*, Jan. 15, 1944, 4; "PTC Employees," Nov. 20, 1943, folder Local 234 Aug.–Dec. 1943, box 81, TWUP.

39. Untitled speech, Dec. 10, 1943, memo to D. L. MacMahon, Dec. 17, 1943, folder Local 234 Aug.–Dec. 1943, box 81, TWUP.

40. Roberts, "A History and Analysis," 184; Police Report, Mar. 10, 1944, sworn statements of Mar. 6 and Mar. 4, 1944, folder PTC Employees Election for Union Bargaining Agent and Election Day Mar. 14, 1944, etc., box A-5637, Detective Division Case Files, City Archives; statements of McDevitt and Quill, Mar. 1944, folder Local 234 Mar.–May 1944, box 81, TWUP; Hill, *Black Labor*, 293.

The Brotherhood of Railroad Trainmen, whose bylaws restricted membership to white males, participated in the campaign for a short time but dropped out after it became apparent that they could not win.

41. "The P.R.T. Employees' Union," n.d., folder Local 234 Mar.–May 1944, box 81, TWUP; *Pennsylvania Labor Record*, Nov. 19, 1943, 1; folder Evening Bulletin Transit Collection, Urban Archives; *Transport Workers Bulletin*, Aug. 1943, 6.

For more on labor and anticommunism, see Rosswurm, *CIO's Left-Led Unions*; Jenkins, *Cold War at Home*.

42. *PM*, Aug. 6, 1944, 3; Meier and Rudwick, "Communist Unions," 184, 187; Hill, *Black Labor*, 292; "United & Alert—For Victory!" n.d., folder Local 234 Aug.–Dec. 1943, box 81, TWUP; clippings in folder Evening Bulletin Transit Collection, Urban Archives.

43. *Philadelphia Tribune*, editorial, Mar. 11, 1944, folder Local 234 Mar.–May 1944, box 81, TWUP; *Philadelphia Tribune*, Mar. 25, 1944, 4; clippings from *Philadelphia Afro-American* and unnamed and undated newspaper in Scrapbook of Clippings, 1943–45, box 52, PNAACP.

44. G. James Fleming to Malcolm Ross, July 8, 1944, folder FEPC vs. PTC and PRT, box 1, PFEPC; "Philadelphia Transportation Company Employees' Strike," Aug. 7, 1944, folder Philadelphia Transportation Company Strike, Review and Analysis—Mitchell-Davis, box 453, FFEPC; Roberts, "A History and Analysis," 177–78; Rohrbeck, *Street Railway Buildings*.

There was also a smattering of "no union" votes, but they amounted to only about 2 percent of the total.

45. *PM*, Aug. 6, 1944, 3, Aug. 4, 1944, 4; Meier and Rudwick, "Communist Unions," 191.

46. Clippings in folder Evening Bulletin Transit Collection, Urban Archives; *Transport Workers Bulletin*, July 1944, 9; *Prospectus*, Nov. 1945, folder 1, box 137, Albert Greenfield Papers, Historical Society of Pennsylvania.

47. *Philadelphia Evening Bulletin*, Aug. 9, 1944, 3; *Pennsylvania Labor Record*, Aug. 18, 1944, 7; FBI testimony of James Fitzsimon, Aug. 8, 1944, folder Local 234 June–Aug. 1944, box 81, TWUP; Meier and Rudwick, "Communist Unions," 192; William Richter to Franklin Roosevelt, Jan. 6, 1944, folder PTC and PRT, box 1, PFEPC.

Chapter Six

1. Clipping in file Clips *Bulletin* Strikes—Transit—1944 Phila.—Aug. 1–5, box 227A, MC; *PM*, Aug. 6, 1944, 19.

2. Ibid.

3. Clipping in file Clips *Bulletin* Strikes—Transit—1944 Phila.—Miscel., box 227A, MC; *PM*, Aug. 4, 1944, 4.

4. *PM*, Aug. 4, 1944, 4.

5. Ibid.

6. *Philadelphia Evening Bulletin*, Aug. 1, 1944, 3.

7. *Pennsylvania Labor Record*, Aug. 18, 1944, 7; *New York Times*, Aug. 3, 1944, 32; *Daily Worker*, Aug. 4, 1944, 2, Aug. 5, 1944, 4; *Philadelphia Tribune*, Aug. 5, 1944, 20; *Philadelphia Afro-American*, Aug. 12, 1944, 12; *PM*, Oct. 16, 1944, 9; *Transport Workers Bulletin*, Aug. 1944, 2.

8. Mr. Will Maslow, director of field operations, Aug. 4, 1944, folder Philadelphia Transportation Company Strike, Review and Analysis—Mitchell-Davis, box 453, FFEPC; Winkler, "Philadelphia Transit Strike of 1944," 81; *New York Times*, Aug. 2, 1944, 19.

9. *PM*, Aug. 6, 1944, 4, 3; untitled and undated document, Archivist's personal folder TWU: Philadelphia, James Fitzsimon to F. J. Biddle, Aug. 1, 1944, folder Local 234 June–Aug. 1944, box 81, TWUP; Hill, *Black Labor*, 301, 298.

10. Meier and Rudwick, "Communist Unions," 192–93; *PM*, Aug. 6, 1944, 4; undated clipping from *Philadelphia Record* in Scrapbook of Clippings, 1943–45, box 52, PNAACP; memo for the provost marshal general, Aug. 10, 1944, folder "Philadelphia Transportation Company," box 803, AR; Hill, *Black Labor*, 420; "Philly Transit Workers Start Back to Jobs as Army Takes Over," Aug. 4, 1944, folder Local 234 June–Aug. 1944, TWUP; J. Edgar Hoover to Jonathan Daniels, Aug. 1, 1944, Office File 4245g, FDRP.

11. Labor Squad reports, July and Aug. 1944, folder Mayor's Papers 1943—Police Department, box A407, Bernard Samuel Papers, City Archives; *Philadelphia Inquirer*, Aug. 7, 1944, 4, Aug. 6, 1944, 3; *Daily Worker*, Aug. 5, 1944, 4; "Philadelphia Law Enforcement and Negro-White Relations," n.d., folder Phil. 1944 USO Study, box 66, National Urban League; Brown, *Law Administration*, 100–101; *Pennsylvania Labor Record*, Aug. 18, 1944, 7.

12. *Congressional Record* (Aug. 7, 1944), 90, pt. 10:A3530–31; FBI statement of Douglas MacMahon, Aug. 8, 1944, folder Local 234 June–Aug. 1944, box 81, TWUP; J. Edgar

Hoover to Jonathan Daniels, Aug. 8, 1944, Office File 4245g, FDRP; Mr. Will Maslow, director of field operations, Aug. 4, 1944, folder Philadelphia Transportation Company Strike, Review and Analysis—Mitchell-Davis, box 453, FFEPC.

13. Bracey and Meier, *Papers of the NAACP*, Part 13, Series A, reel 19; Carolyn Moore to Roy Wilkins, Oct. 11, 1944, folder Philadelphia, PA Rapid Transit Strike 1944–45, box A468, NNAACP; A. J. Stoddard to William Henry Welsh, Aug. 10, 1944, folder 64–21, box 64, FCP; clipping from unnamed and undated newspaper in Scrapbook of Clippings, 1943–45, box 52, PNAACP.

14. For more on how management manipulated workers' racism, see Sugrue, "Segmented Work," 388–406. Eric Arnesen raises similar issues when he asks who gets to decide who is white. See "Whiteness and the Historians' Imagination," 18.

15. *PM*, Aug. 3, 1944, 10, Aug. 2, 1944, 10; *Daily Worker*, Aug. 7, 1944, 2; *New York Times*, Aug. 2, 1944, 19.

16. *New York Times*, Aug. 7, 1944, 14; *Daily Worker*, Aug. 10, 1944, 7, Aug. 11, 1944, 6; *Philadelphia Evening Bulletin*, Aug. 9, 1944, 3; *Philadelphia Inquirer*, Aug. 2, 1944, 12; White, *A Rising Wind*, 153–55.

17. William Davis to Franklin Roosevelt, Aug. 3, 1944, President's Executive Order, Aug. 3, 1944, Office File 4451, FDRP; *New York Times*, Aug. 4, 1944, 18; clipping in file Clips *Bulletin* Strikes—Transit—1944 Phila.—Aug. 6 and later, box 227A, MC; Winkler, "Philadelphia Transit Strike of 1944," 83.

18. Clippings in file Clips *Bulletin* Strikes—Transit—1944 Phila.—Aug. 6 and later, file Clips *Bulletin* Strikes—Transit—1944 Phila.—Miscel., box 227A, MC; *New York Times*, Aug. 4, 1944, 18, Aug. 6, 1944, 30; *United States v. McMenamin.*

19. *PM*, Aug. 4, 1944, 2.

20. *Chicago Defender*, Aug. 12, 1944, 4; "FEPC Faces a Crisis," Sept. 1944, folder Philadelphia Transit Strike, 1944, box 15, FOR; clippings from *Philadelphia Record*, n.d., and Aug. 2, 1944, in Scrapbook of Clippings, 1943–45, box 52, PNAACP; *PM*, Aug. 4, 1944, 2; *Daily Worker*, Aug. 5, 1944, 2; "Intelligence Estimate of Philadelphia Transit Company Strike," Aug. 2, 1944, folder "Philadelphia Transportation Company," box 803, AR; Hill, *Black Labor*, 296–97.

For more on how the Euro-American working class cemented its whiteness in the World War II era, see Gerstle, *American Crucible*, 3–13; Nelson, *Divided We Stand*, xxxiv, 158–59; Barrett and Roediger, "Inbetween Peoples."

This white labor discourse has resonated throughout American history. For insightful analyses, see Foner, *Free Soil*; Foner, *Reconstruction*; Roediger, *Wages of Whiteness*; Ignatiev, *How the Irish Became White*.

21. Employment poster, Oct. 1943, G. James Fleming to Will Maslow, June 30, 1944, folder Philadelphia Transportation Company 3-BR-246 (Philadelphia, PA), box 343, FFEPC; Jackson, *Crabgrass Frontier*, 195–219; *Trade Union News*, Aug. 11, 1944, 6.

22. Alvin Paine to Governor Martin, Aug. 1, 1944, container 16, EMP.

23. *Philadelphia Inquirer*, Aug. 3, 1944, 4; Helena O'Donnell to Department of Labor,

Aug. 4, 1944, Office File 4451, J. Edgar Hoover to Jonathan Daniels, Aug. 16, 1944, Office File 4245g, FDRP; clippings in SEPTA (Southeast Pennsylvania Transit Authority) Collection, Urban Archives; G. James Fleming to George Crockett, Jan. 4, 1944, folder FEPC vs. PTC and PRT, box 1, PFEPC; *Daily Worker*, Aug. 5, 1944, 2; clipping from *Philadelphia Record*, Aug. 2, 1944, in Scrapbook of Clippings, 1943–45, box 52, PNAACP; memo for the provost marshal general, Aug. 10, 1944, folder "Philadelphia Transportation Company," box 803, AR; police report, Aug. 9, 1944, untitled folder, box A5637, Philadelphia Police Department Records, City Archives.

For more on the potentially explosive meeting of black men and white women at work, see Boris, "You Wouldn't Want One of 'Em Dancing with Your Wife"; Boyle, "The Kiss"; Nelson, "Organized Labor."

24. Maurice Fagan to Dear Friend, Dec. 24, 1943, folder 30, box 1, FCP; G. James Fleming to Will Maslow, Nov. 19, 1943, folder FEPC vs. PTC and PRT, box 1, PFEPC; clipping from *Philadelphia Record*, n.d., in Scrapbook of Clippings, 1944–52, box 53, PNAACP; *Philadelphia Afro-American*, Aug. 12, 1944, 12; *Daily Worker*, Aug. 4, 1944, 2.

Similar issues plagued other points of contact. The United Service Organizations, for example, provided the stage for a number of clashes over relations with white women. See Lovelace, "Facing Change in Wartime Philadelphia."

Commentators, particularly those sympathetic to African Americans, widely noted the difference between what blacks said they wanted and what whites thought blacks wanted. See Logan, *What the Negro Wants*, especially the essay by W. E. B. Du Bois; Myrdal, *An American Dilemma*.

25. Bartley, *Rise of Massive Resistance*.

26. Clippings from unnamed and undated newspapers in Scrapbook of Clippings, 1943–45, box 52, PNAACP; *Philadelphia Evening Bulletin*, Aug. 13, 1944, 1, 3; "News of Public Opinion Surveys," Oct. 22, 1944, folder Urban League of Philadelphia Equal Job Opportunity 1944, 1960, box 2, PUL.

27. WCAU radio address, Aug. 5, 1944, folder Local 234 June–Aug. 1944, box 81, TWUP; *Philadelphia Inquirer*, Oct. 5, 1944, 10; clipping from *Philadelphia Record*, n.d., in Scrapbook of Clippings, 1943–45, box 52, PNAACP.

28. *Philadelphia Inquirer*, Aug. 25, 1944, 6, Aug. 8, 1944, 6; memo for the provost marshal general, Aug. 10, 1944, folder "Philadelphia Transportation Company," box 803, AR; clippings in file for James McMenamin, EBM; Philleo Nash to Jonathan Daniels, Aug. 22, 1944, Office File 4245g, FDRP; James Letcher Caruthers to commanding officer, labor squad, Aug. 23, 1944, folder PTC Strike—Aug. 1944, box A5637, Philadelphia Police Department Records, City Archives; Meier and Rudwick, "Communist Unions," 192; clippings in file Clips *Bulletin* Strikes—Transit—1946 Phila., file Clips *Bulletin* Strikes—Transit—1949, Phila Feb. 11–14, file Clips *Bulletin* Strikes—Transit—1950–1952 Phila., file Clips *Bulletin* Strikes—Transit—1953 Phila., file Clips *Bulletin* Strikes—Transit—1955 Phila., file Clips *Bulletin* Strikes—Transit—1955–59 Phila., box 227A, MC.

29. Clipping in file for James McMenamin, EBM; *New York Times*, Aug. 7, 1944, 24;

Philleo Nash to Jonathan Daniels, Aug. 25, 1944, Office File 4245g, FDRP; *Daily Worker*, ·
Aug. 4, 1944, 2; *Philadelphia Evening Bulletin*, Aug. 2, 1944, 1.

30. Clipping from *Philadelphia Record*, n.d., in Scrapbook of Clippings, 1943–45,
box 52, PNAACP; *Philadelphia Inquirer*, Aug. 2, 1944, 3; "Philadelphia Transportation
Company—Developments—1000–1500," Aug. 4, 1944, folder Philadelphia Transporta-
tion Company, box 803, AR; *New York Times*, Aug. 8, 1944, 19; Report of Cornelius
Golightly, Aug. 7, 1944, folder Philadelphia Transportation Company Strike, Review and
Analysis—Mitchell-Davis, box 453, FFEPC.

31. Clipping in file Clips *Bulletin* Strikes—Transit—1944 Phila.—Aug. 1–5, box 227A,
MC; *Philadelphia Inquirer*, Aug. 8, 1944, 8; clipping in unnamed and undated newspaper
in Scrapbook of Clippings, 1943–45, box 52, PNAACP; *Daily Worker*, Aug. 9, 1944, 5; J.
Edgar Hoover to Jonathan Daniels, Aug. 4, 1944, Office File 4245g, FDRP.

32. Clipping from *Pittsburgh Courier*, n.d., clipping from unnamed and undated newspaper in Scrapbook of Clippings, 1943–45, box 52, PNAACP; John Davis to NAACP, n.d.,
folder Philadelphia, PA Rapid Transit Strike 1944–45, box A468, NNAACP.

33. "Analysis of Editorial Opinion No. 62," n.d., Office File 4245g, FDRP; "The North
and Its Negroes!" Aug. 20, 1944, folder FEPC Correspondence, Aug.–Dec. 1944, box 111,
Richard Russell Papers, Athens, Ga.; Sitkoff, *A New Deal for Blacks*, 104, 293; *Congressional Record* (Aug. 9, 1944), 90, pt. 5:6804–809.

34. William Fogg to Richard Russell, Sept. 18, 1944, folder FEPC Correspondence,
Aug.–Dec. 1944, box 111, Richard Russell Papers, Athens, Ga.

35. *Nation*, Aug. 12, 1944, 172; *New York Post*, Aug. 4, 1944, folder Local 234 Clippings,
box 81, TWUP.

36. Bracey and Meier, *Papers of the NAACP*, Part 13, Series A, reel 19; *Daily Worker*,
Aug. 10, 1944, 7; clippings from unnamed and undated newspapers in Scrapbook of
Clippings, 1943–45, box 52, PNAACP; Franklin, *Education of Black Philadelphia*, 161.

37. *Philadelphia Inquirer*, Aug. 5, 1944, 6, Aug. 4, 1944, 6; *New York Times*, Aug. 5,
1944, 10; "Editor," Aug. 5, 1944, Office File 4245g, FDRP.

38. "Philadelphia Answers the Enemy's Challenge!" Aug. 6, 1944, folder Local 234
June–Aug. 1944, clipping from unnamed newspaper, Aug. 7, 1944, folder Local 234
Clippings File, box 81, TWUP; *Daily Worker*, Aug. 14, 1944, 7, Aug. 5, 1944, 2, Aug. 9, 1944,
9, Aug. 3, 1944, 2; *Philadelphia Evening Bulletin*, Aug. 4, 1944, 2; Jewish War Veterans to
Edward Martin, Aug. 3, 1944, container 16, EMP; "Report on Activities of Various Organizations to Allay Possible Racial Difficulties in P.T.C. Strike," Aug. 5, 1944, folder "Philadelphia Transportation Company," box 803, AR.

39. *Philadelphia Inquirer*, Aug. 3, 1944. 8, Aug. 5, 1944, 6.

40. "Philadelphia Report on the Transportation Strike," n.d., folder Philadelphia, PA
June–Aug. 1944, box C167, "N.A.A.C.P. Urges F.D.R. Stand against Strikers," Aug. 1, 1944,
folder Philadelphia, PA Rapid Transit Strike 1944–45, box A468, NNAACP; "Colored
American" to President Roosevelt, Aug. 1, 1944, folder Newspaper Clippings and Letters
from Public PTC Case, box 3, PFEPC; Louise Startsman to Frank McNamee, regional

director, WMC, n.d., folder Strikes, box 2370, Philadelphia War Manpower Commission Papers, National Archives, Philadelphia branch.

41. Paul McNutt to Walter White, n.d., box A468, NNAACP; *Daily Worker*, Aug. 8, 1944, 3.

42. *Philadelphia Afro-American*, Aug. 5, 1944, 3, Aug. 12, 1944, 19; Spaulding, "Philadelphia's Hate Strike," 281; *New York Times*, Aug. 2, 1944, 19, 1; clippings in file Clips *Bulletin* Strikes—Transit—1944 Phila.—Aug. 1–5, box 227A, MC; J. Edgar Hoover to Jonathan Daniels, Aug. 2, 1944, Office File 4245g, FDRP; *Philadelphia Evening Bulletin*, Aug. 2, 1944, 3; Brown, *Law Administration*, 125–27; *Pittsburgh Courier*, Aug. 12, 1944, 4; report from Wharton Centre worker, n.d., file 252, Wharton Centre Papers, Urban Archives.

For examples of war-era violence in other cities, see Sugrue, *Origins of the Urban Crisis*, 17–88; Nelson, "Organized Labor"; Brandt, *Harlem at War*.

43. Spaulding, "Philadelphia's Hate Strike," 301; Weckler and Weaver, *Negro Platform Workers*, 15; clipping in file Clips *Bulletin* Strikes—Transit—1944 Phila.—Aug. 1–5, box 227A, MC; "Attention Citizens!" n.d., folder Philadelphia, PA Rapid Transit Strike 1944–45, box A468, "Philadelphia Report on the Transportation Strike," n.d., folder Philadelphia, PA June–Aug. 1944, box C167, NNAACP; Raymond Pace Alexander, Theodore Spaulding, and Carolyn Moore to Edward Martin, Aug. 2, 1944, container 16, EMP; *PM*, Aug. 6, 1944, 5.

44. Clipping in file Clips *Bulletin* Strikes—Transit—1944 Phila.—Aug. 6 and later, box 227A, MC; *Daily Worker*, Aug. 8, 1944, 2; Max Yergan to Michael Quill, Aug. 8, 1944, folder Local 234 June–Aug. 1944, box 81, TWUP; National Urban League press release, Aug. 14, 1944, folder News Releases 1942–44, box 34, National Urban League Papers, Library of Congress; *New York Times*, Aug. 14, 1944, 15; *Philadelphia Tribune*, Aug. 12, 1944, 4; *PM*, Aug. 3, 1944, 12; *Philadelphia Afro-American*, Aug. 12, 1944, 10.

45. *Chicago Defender*, Aug. 19, 1944, 3; *Daily Worker*, Aug. 17, 1944, 8.

46. *Philadelphia Record*, Oct. 5, 1944, 4; *Daily Worker*, Aug. 3, 1944, 2, Aug. 11, 1944, 6, Aug. 5, 1944, 2, 1; Federated Press articles, Aug. 10, 1944, Aug. 3, 1944, folder Local 234 June–Aug. 1944, box 81, TWUP; John Friedrich to C. O. Troop, Aug. 8, 1944, container 16, EMP; "Intelligence Estimate of Philadelphia Transit Company Strike," Aug. 2, 1944, folder "Philadelphia Transportation Company," box 803, AR; Bracey and Meier, *Papers of the NAACP*, Part 13, Series A, reel 19.

47. Francis Biddle to Franklin Roosevelt, Jan. 29, 1943, folder Civil Rights/Fair Employment, box Aliens and Immigration—Correspondence: A–H, container 1, Francis Biddle Papers, Hyde Park, N.Y.

48. James Bristol to A. J. Muste, Aug. 28, 1944, folder Philadelphia Transit Strike, 1944, box 15, FOR; Philleo Nash to Jonathan Daniels, Aug. 25, 1944, Office File 4245g, FDRP; *Philadelphia Inquirer*, Aug. 19, 1944, 5; *South Philadelphia American*, Sept. 8, 1944, 2, Sept. 15, 1944, 2, Oct. 22, 1944, 2, Oct. 29, 1944, 2, Nov. 5, 1944, 8; late summer and fall 1944 editions of *Kensington News*, *Kensington Critic*, and *Ordine Nuovo*; Miller, "The Negro in Pennsylvania Politics," 297–98.

49. *Jewish Times*, Nov. 17, 1944, 21, Aug. 11, 1944, 11; Fuchs, *Political Behavior of American Jews*, 78; Philleo Nash to Jonathan Daniels, Aug. 25, 1944, Office File 4245g, FDRP.

For examples of ethnic newspapers circulating in Philadelphia during the war, see *Unione, Italian Tribune, Gaelic American, Irish World, American Industrial Liberator, Ordine Nuovo, Kensington News, Kensington Critic*, and *South Philadelphia American*.

50. Gallup, *Gallup Poll*, 467–68; Grove, "Decline of the Republican Machine," 396, 899.

51. O'Neill, *A Democracy at War*, 398; *Evening Bulletin Almanac* (1946), 429; *Philadelphia Tribune*, Apr. 15, 1944, 4, July 8, 1944, 4; Fauset, "Philadelphia's Unfinished Business," 140; Bracey and Meier, *Papers of the NAACP*, Part 18, Series C, reel 30; Grove, "Decline of the Republican Machine," 404, 201; Miller, "The Negro in Pennsylvania Politics," 281, 284; Shover, "Ethnicity and Religion in Philadelphia Politics."

Chapter Seven

1. Dickinson, "Story of 'Busted Block,'" 33.

2. Ibid., 34–35.

3. Ibid.

4. "The *Real* Story about the Big City," Feb. 6, 1959, folder Urban League of Philadelphia Equal Job Opportunity 1944, 1960, box 2, PUL; Dickinson, "Great Industrial Variety," 4–5; Arnold, "Building the Beloved Community," 198; Jon Birger, "Race, Reaction, and Reform," 181.

The seminal work on racial conflict in the neighborhoods of the urban North is Hirsch, *Making the Second Ghetto*. See also Hirsch, "Massive Resistance," Sugrue, "Crabgrass-Roots Politics" and *Origins of the Urban Crisis*; Gerstle, "Race and the Myth of the Liberal Consensus"; Hirsch and Mohl, *Urban Policy in Twentieth-Century America*; Bauman, Biles, and Szylvian, *From Tenements to the Taylor Homes*; Rieder, *Canarsie*; Keating, *Suburban Racial Dilemma*.

5. Philadelphia Housing Association, *Issues*, Nov.–Dec. 1945, 1–2; Anne Coyle to Dorothy Montgomery, Dec. 13, 1946, folder 319, box 54, HADV.

The postwar housing shortage hit other cities too. See O'Neill, *American High*, 12–13; Wright, *Building the Dream*, 242–43; Jackson, *A Place Called Home*, 244.

6. "Some Basic Facts concerning the Negro Population of Philadelphia," n.d., folder Housing Department, Non-white Housing 1939, 1953–60, box 10, "The *Real* Story about the Big City," Feb. 6, 1959, folder Urban League of Philadelphia Equal Job Opportunity 1944, 1960, box 2, PUL; Philadelphia Housing Association, *Philadelphia's Negro Population*, 17, 7; Dickinson, "Calm Philadelphia," 31; Nelson, "Race and Class Consciousness," 145; Franklin, *Education of Black Philadelphia*, 152; Strange, "Blacks and Philadelphia Politics," 127–28; Hershberg et al., "A Tale of Three Cities," 479–80.

7. Rothman, *Philadelphia Government, 1956*, 3; Franklin, *Education of Black Philadelphia*, 152; Commission on Race and Housing, *Where Shall We Live?*, 53; Bressler, "The Myers' Case," 127.

8. "The *Real* Story about the Big City," Feb. 6, 1959, folder Urban League of Philadelphia Equal Job Opportunity 1944, 1960, box 2, PUL; Rapkin and Grigsby, *Demand for Housing*, 5, 78; Dickinson, "Great Industrial Variety," 3; Scranton and Licht, *Work Sights*, 267; Scranton, "Large Firms and Industrial Restructuring," 419–65; Countryman, "Civil Rights and Black Power," 80–81.

9. Willis, *Cecil's City*, 83–85; file titled Ku Klux Klan, EBM; Lees, "How Philadelphia Stopped a Race Riot."

10. Lees, "How Philadelphia Stopped a Race Riot."

11. Ibid.

12. Ibid.

13. "Report on the Contacts with the Olney Garden Apartments," Jan. 8, 1955, folder Levittown Housing Proj., 1952–55, *J. Ralph Pearson and Otillia Pearson v. Olney Gardens, Inc.*, n.d., folder Levittown Housing Project—Miscellany, box 12, PNAACP.

14. Chafe, *Civilities and Civil Rights*; Binzen, *Whitetown U.S.A.*, 142, 86, 110–12, 100.

15. File titled Ku Klux Klan, EBM; clippings in folder A, box Research and Investigation Newspaper Clippings, JCRC; *Philadelphia Tribune*, Sept. 3, 1946, 1, Sept. 7, 1946, 1, 2, 4, Sept. 10, 1946, 1, 3, Aug. 3, 1946, 2, 4.

Historian Richard Dalfiume found that the Klan was on the rise across America in the postwar years. See Dalfiume, *Desegregation of the U.S. Armed Forces*, 133–34.

16. File titled Ku Klux Klan, EBM; *Philadelphia Tribune*, Sept. 3, 1946, 15, June 18, 1952, 3; Weiler, *Philadelphia*, 134–36; Bracey, Harley, and Meier, *Papers of the NAACP*, Part 26, Series B, reel 10; William Welsh to Hubley Owen, Mar. 11, 1943, folder 23, box 1, FCP; "Organized Anti-Semitic Groups or Activities in Philadelphia and Their Leaders," n.d., folder Anti-Semitism, box Research and Investigations, JCRC.

Research for this study uncovered only one instance of Klan activity directed against non–African Americans. In Chambersburg, the KKK told veterans they could not buy houses because while they were overseas, "the Jews came in and bought up all the property, and ran rents and prices sky high." Even in this case, though, Klansmen also told veterans that they would not find any jobs because "a Negro already has [them all]."

17. Beers, *Pennsylvania Politics*, 167–68; file titled Ku Klux Klan, EBM; Jenkins, *Cold War at Home*, 54; clipping in Book 1, box 21 Scrapbooks, JCRC.

18. Clipping in folder A, box Research and Investigation Newspaper Clippings, JCRC.

19. Rapkin and Grigsby, *Demand for Housing*, 140–41, 54, 79, 116–17; clipping from unnamed newspaper, June 16, 1945, in Scrapbook of Clippings, 1943–45, box 52, PNAACP.

20. Philadelphia Housing Association, *Philadelphia's Negro Population*, 55–56.

21. Philadelphia Housing Association, *Issues*, Oct. 1944, 2; "Negro Housing," Nov. 15, 1946, folder 259, box 47, HADV; clipping from unnamed and undated newspaper in Scrapbook of Clippings, 1944–52, box 53, NAACP press release, May 5, 1956, folder 196, box 9, PNAACP; "Some Basic Facts concerning the Negro Population of Philadelphia," n.d., folder Housing Department, Non-white Housing 1939, 1953–60, box 10, PUL; Rap-

kin and Grigsby, *Demand for Housing*, 74–75; Gans, *Levittowners*, 379; Polenberg, *One Nation Divisible*, 152; Contosta, *Suburb in the City*, 160–263.

In examining the expansion of white suburbs, other scholars have stressed more heavily the role of government agencies in promoting segregation in urban America. They have pointed to redlining, discriminatory federal loans, and other practices that put the government in support of segregation. This study does not not disagree with their interpretation so much as it places a greater emphasis on the part played by ordinary people in creating a segregated housing market. For some examples of this literature, see Jackson, *Crabgrass Frontier*, 191–225; Hirsch, *Making the Second Ghetto*, 245–54; Hirsch, "With or without Jim Crow," 241–49; Radford, "Federal Government and Housing"; Hirsch, "Choosing Segregation"; and Mohl, "Planned Destruction."

22. "Report to the Committee on Race Relations," 1951, Annual Reports, Minutes for Committee on Race Relations, Feb. 6, 1951, binder Apr. 1950–Mar. 1969, box 3, SOFP; Polenberg, *One Nation Divisible*, 152–53; clipping from *Philadelphia Evening Bulletin*, Feb. 23, 1948, in book 1, box 21 Scrapbooks, JCRC; Commission on Race and Housing, *Where Shall We Live?*, 27; Clark, *Ghetto Game*, 30, 110; Ley, *Black Inner City*, 26–29; Binzen, *Whitetown, U.S.A.*; correspondent to Congress of Racial Equality, Apr. 11, 1955, folder CORE, box 2, Congress of Racial Equality Papers, Swarthmore College.

23. U.S. Bureau of the Census, *Population and Housing* (1942), 4–125; U.S. Bureau of the Census, *Census Tract Statistics* (1952), 8–56.

These population numbers are somewhat understated because by the mid-twentieth century many families of European descent had lived in the United States long enough to be classified as "native white" rather than Italian or Irish. Still, these numbers well represent the trends in Philadelphia's population movements.

24. Smaller numbers of Philadelphians from these groups also moved across the Delaware River to New Jersey's Gloucester, Burlington, and Camden counties.

The reconstruction of Philadelphia's postwar ethnic geography presented here draws on census returns of 1940 and 1950, data that were combined with census maps and maps of Philadelphia's neighborhoods. For the neighborhood maps, see Muller, Meyer, and Cybriwsky, *Metropolitan Philadelphia*, 13; Miller, Vogel, and Davis, *Philadelphia Stories*, 4; Southeast Pennsylvania Transit Authority, *Official Philadelphia Transit and Street Map* and *Official Suburban Transit and Street Map*.

25. Former Levittown website, <http://www.levittownpa.org/Levittown.html>; U.S. Bureau of the Census, *Census Tracts* (1962), 21–94; Bressler, "The Myers' Case," 127.

Kenneth Jackson points out that during this era, construction innovations drove suburbanization by transforming homebuilding from a craft into a mass industry. More than anyone, the Levitts perfected that industry. See Jackson, *Crabgrass Frontier*, 125–27.

26. Rapkin and Grigsby, *Demand for Housing*, 120; Arnold, "Building the Beloved Community," 173; Bressler, "The Myers' Case," 140.

Levitt always claimed that as a Jewish liberal he had great concern for discrimination in America, but Levitt and Sons did not sell a home to an African American family until

1960, when a lawsuit forced their hand. They had been selling homes for thirteen years at that point.

27. *Philadelphia Tribune*, May 31, 1952, 4, Sept. 15, 1951, 2, May 31, 1952, 4; Annual Report, 1946, box 7, news release, Apr. 2, 1946, folder 283, box 14, Joseph Hunter to Committee on Law and Order, Mar. 2, 1959, folder 198, box 9, clipping from *Philadelphia Afro-American*, n.d., in Scrapbook of Clippings, 1944–52, box 53, PNAACP; "Report to the Committee on Race Relations," 1951, folder Annual Reports, box 3, SOFP; Arnold, "Building the Beloved Community," 186; Rapkin and Grigsby, *Demand for Housing*, ix.

28. File titled Ku Klux Klan, EBM; Bressler, "The Myers' Case," 127–41; Polenberg, *One Nation Divisible*, 162.

29. Bressler, "The Myers' Case," 126–41.

30. Ibid.

31. Former Levittown website, <http://www.levittownpa.org/Levittown.html>; Gans, *Levittowners*, 23–24, 404–5, 373–76, 404.

32. Gans, *Levittowners*, 372–73, 378–79, 404.

33. *Philadelphia Tribune*, Nov. 4, 1946, 4, Apr. 29, 1950, 4; file titled Clark, Joseph Sill, Jr.—Housing, EBM.

34. Clark and Clark, "Rally and Relapse," 651–57; Morris, *Richardson Dilworth Story*, 101, 87; *Philadelphia Tribune*, Nov. 10, 1951, 4; Reichley, *Art of Government*, 70; Beers, *Pennsylvania Government*, 193–207.

35. Bauman, *Public Housing*, 118–23, 160; Hirsch, *Making the Second Ghetto*; *Philadelphia Tribune*, Feb. 14, 1950, 3; Birger, "Race, Reaction, and Reform," 181.

36. Arnold, "Building the Beloved Community," 182–83; clipping from *Philadelphia Afro-American*, n.d., in Scrapbook of Clippings, 1944–52, box 53, PNAACP; Bauman, *Public Housing*, 128, 169; Luconi, *From Paesani to White Ethnics*, 127; *Greater Northeast News*, June 22, 1950, 1; file titled Clark, Joseph Sill, Jr.—Housing, EBM.

37. *Suburban Press*, Nov. 16, 1950, 1, Nov. 30, 1950, 1.

38. *Suburban Press*, Nov. 30, 1950, 1, 4; Bauman, *Public Housing*, 164, 158.

39. Bauman, *Public Housing*, 163, 158; *Philadelphia Tribune*, May 6, 1950, 1, 2, May 20, 1950, 1; file titled Clark, Joseph Sill, Jr.—Housing, EBM.

40. Petshek, *Challenge of Urban Reform*, 157; file titled Clark, Joseph Sill, Jr.—Housing, EBM; Bauman, *Public Housing*, 118, 165; Arnold, "Building the Beloved Community," 184; Clark, *Irish in Philadelphia*, 159–60.

41. Palmer, "Philadelphia Labor Market in 1944," 5; Miller, Vogel, and Davis, *Philadelphia Stories*, 161, 192, 117; Population and Economic Research Advisory Committee, *Labor Force and Employment Estimates*, 9; Adams, *Philadelphia*, 31; Scranton, "Large Firms," 420.

For a similar story of World War II's transitory effects on the economy, see Miller, *Irony of Victory*.

42. Population and Economic Research Advisory Committee, *Labor Force and Employment Estimates*, 9; Adams, *Philadelphia*, 17; Miller, Vogel, and Davis, *Philadelphia Stories*, 277; Dickinson, "Great Industrial Variety," 4–5; Bauman, *Public Housing*, 162.

For more on this vision of a postwar industrial garden, see Self, *American Babylon*, 23–60.

43. Adams, *Philadelphia*, 19; Licht, *Getting Work*, 55.

44. Zieger, *CIO*, 212–52; Adams, *Philadelphia*, 31–32; Miller, Vogel, and Davis, *Philadelphia Stories*, 177; Scranton and Licht, *Work Sights*, 257–65.

45. Sugrue, *Origins of the Urban Crisis*, 156; Fones-Wolf, *Selling Free Enterprise*; Dickinson, "Great Industrial Variety," 3; Miller, Vogel, and Davis, *Philadelphia Stories*, 189, 162.

For a similar experience in Detroit, see Sugrue, *Origins of the Urban Crisis*, 153–77.

46. Brown, *Law Administration*, 48; Scranton and Licht, *Work Sights*, 244–46; "Growth of Philadelphia's Negro Population," n.d., folder Urban League of Philadelphia Research Department Statistical Reports and Graphs 1927–61, box 12, PUL; Bauman, Hummon, and Muller, "Public Housing," 454–55.

47. Arnold, "Building the Beloved Community," 155; Commission on Law and Social Action, n.d., folder FEPC, box 14, FOR; O'Donnell, "Pennsylvania's Self-Survey."

48. Bauman, *Public Housing*, 161; Binzen, *Whitetown, U.S.A.*; Adams, *Philadelphia*, 25; minutes from Committee on School and Community Tensions, folder 138, box 8, PUL.

49. "The *Real* Story about the Big City," Feb. 6, 1959, folder Urban League of Philadelphia Equal Job Opportunity 1944, 1960, box 2, PUL Papers; Bauman, Hummon, and Muller, "Public Housing," 456–57; Bauman, *Public Housing*, 84, 118, 154.

There is a substantial body of work on the impact of urban renewal on African Americans, but the starting point is Hirsch, *Making the Second Ghetto*.

50. Clipping from unnamed newspaper, Nov. 11, 1944, in Scrapbook of Clippings, 1943–45, box 52, PNAACP; Willis, *Cecil's City*, 65; Arnold, "Building the Beloved Community," 237.

For more on the department store campaign, see Cooper, "Limits of Persuasion."

51. Marjorie Swann to Dear Friends, n.d., folder 58-5, box 58, FCP.

On Communism in the Philadelphia NAACP, see Bracey, Harley, and Meier, *Papers of the NAACP*, Part 26, Series B, reel 10; Countryman, "Civil Rights and Black Power," 51–83.

52. "Report for Charles Shorter," Sept. 25, 1946, folder 5, FCP; untitled document, Feb. 5, 1946, "Committee on Fair Employment Practices in Department Stores: Department Store Interview," Jan. 24, 1946, folder Committee on Fair Employment, 1945–1946, box 6, SOFP.

53. Untitled document, Feb. 5, 1946, "Committee on Fair Employment Practices in Department Stores: Department Store Interview," Jan. 15, 1946, folder Committee on Fair Employment, 1945–1946, box 6, SOFP; Muriel to John, June 15, 1949, folder 55-20, FCP.

54. Untitled document, Feb. 5, 1946, "A White Hand—or Black?" Sept. 22, 1945, folder Committee on Fair Employment, 1945–1946, box 6, SOFP.

55. "A White Hand—or Black?" Sept. 22, 1945, "Summary, Negro Sales-Clerk Poll, Philadelphia," n.d., folder Committee on Fair Employment, 1945–1946, box 6, SOFP.

56. "Press Release—Fair Employment Practices in Department Stores Committee," n.d., folder 5, FCP; Arnold, "Building the Beloved Community," 230.

57. Wilson, *Truly Disadvantaged*; Lane, *William Dorsey's Philadelphia*, 363.

Chapter Eight

1. Clippings from *Philadelphia Evening Bulletin*, Feb. 19, 1948, *Philadelphia Daily News*, Feb. 19, 1948, in scrapbook 1, box 21, JCRC.

2. Ibid.

3. Clipping from *Philadelphia Tribune*, Apr. 9, 1949, in scrapbook 1949 Campaign for a FEPC Law, box 21, JCRC; *Philadelphia Tribune*, Nov. 4, 1950, 1.

4. For further examples of more overt racism in the urban North, see Carter, *Politics of Rage*; Garrow, *Bearing the Cross*, 500–549; Sugrue, *Origins of the Urban Crisis*.

For more on the Philadelphia and Pennsylvania FEPC campaigns, see Wolfinger, "'An Equal Opportunity to Make a Living—and a Life'"; Smith and Wolensky, "A Novel Public Policy."

5. Franklin, *Education of Black Philadelphia*, 160–61; Bracey, Harley, and Meier, *Papers of the NAACP*, Part 26, Series B, reel 9; "Minutes of the Board of Directors of the Philadelphia Branch N.A.A.C.P.—November 3, 1944," Nov. 3, 1944, "Report of Chairman of the Board to the Philadelphia Branch—NAACP," Jan. 2, 1945, box 1, clipping from unnamed newspaper, Nov. 1944, in Scrapbook of Clippings, 1943–45, box 52, PNAACP; "The FEPC Faces a Crisis," Sept. 1944, folder Philadelphia transit strike, 1944, box 15, FOR; Wilkerson, *Proceedings*, 8.

6. Untitled speech, Oct. 24, 1944, folder Francis Biddle Papers/Civil Rights/Fair Employment, container 1, Francis Biddle Papers, Hyde Park, N.Y.

There are a number of studies of the FEPC, but for the most detailed treatment of the committee's career, see Reed, *Seedtime*.

7. O'Neill, *A Democracy at War*, 391–92; "NAACP to Intensify Fight for FEPC and Housing," Apr. 2, 1946, folder 283, box 14, PNAACP; *Philadelphia Tribune*, Nov. 17, 1945, 1, Sept. 15, 1945, 4.

8. Dalfiume, *Desegregation of the U.S. Armed Forces*; O'Neill, *American High*, 247–48; Reed, *Seedtime*, 339–43.

9. *Philadelphia Tribune*, Mar. 11, 1950, 1, Dec. 8, 1945, 2, Dec. 3, 1949, 4.

10. Clipping from *PM*, Mar. 15, 1945, in Scrapbook of Clippings 1944–52, box 53, PNAACP; *Philadelphia Tribune*, Feb. 12, 1952, 2, July 12, 1952, 1, Dec. 13, 1949, 2, Feb. 24, 1945, 2, Aug. 4, 1945, 1, July 13, 1946, 3; "Report concerning Present Status of a Federal FEPC Bill," n.d., folder 14, FCP.

New York, Chicago, and other states and cities with stronger progressive political groups overcame such opposition and established fair employment committees anyway. See Graves, *Fair Employment Practice Legislation*; Fleming, "Administration of Fair Employment Practice Programs," 26–29; Gray, *Lobbying Game*, 121.

For a contemporary analysis of Republican racial politics across the nation as it applied to the FEPC, see Aronson and Spiegler, "Does the Republican Party Want the Negro Vote?" 364–68, 411–17.

11. Bracey, Harley, and Meier, *Papers of the NAACP*, Part 26, Series B, reel 9; minutes for Committee on Race Relations, Feb. 6, 1951, in binder Apr. 1950–Mar. 1969, box 3, SOFP; Miller, "The Negro in Pennsylvania Politics," 360.

12. "Proposed Script to Review Activities," n.d., "NAACP Forum of the Air," Aug. 12, 1953, "Council for Equal Job Opportunity: Report to the Membership," Jan. 1951, folder Employment Discrimination 1950–1955, untitled box, JCRC; Clark, *Irish Relations*, 185–86; *Philadelphia Tribune*, Nov. 3, 1945, 1; *Interracial Review*, Nov. 1945, 166, Oct. 1946, 148, July 1949, 102; Report of the Committee on Race Relations, 1949, Annual Reports, box 3, SOFP.

13. Dudziak, *Cold War Civil Rights*; *Philadelphia Tribune*, Apr. 9, 1949, 2, Feb. 21, 1950, 2, Oct. 7, 1947, 2; Reichley, *Art of Government*, 80, 17; clipping in file Clark, Joseph Sill, Jr., EBM.

14. Reichley, *Art of Government*, 72–85; Featherman, "Italian American Voting in Local Elections," 48–49.

Samuel Lubell made a similar argument about the effect of white racism and the politics of the FEPC on the stability of the Democratic Party in *The Future of American Politics*, 82–96. In particular, he noted that as blacks moved to the urban North they strained the economic ties binding the party's constituents together and that Republicans around the country picked up support by opposing the FEPC.

15. Clippings in folder F, box Research and Investigations Newspaper Clippings, clipping from *Philadelphia Tribune*, Jan. 24, 1948, in book 1, box 21 Scrapbooks, JCRC; *Philadelphia Tribune*, June 4, 1946, 1; NAACP news release, May 17, 1946, folder 283, box 14, PNAACP.

16. Clipping from *Philadelphia Tribune*, Mar. 9, 1948, in folder F, box Research and Investigations Newspaper Clippings, JCRC; *Philadelphia Tribune*, Mar. 6, 1948, 1.

17. Jenkins, *Hoods and Shirts*, 208–9, 228, 225; Jeansonne, *Gerald L. K. Smith*; Maurice Fagan to John Sears, Apr. 24, 1942, "Bring the Boys Home," n.d., folder Blue Star Mothers, box Research and Investigation, JCRC.

18. "FEPC Is Communistic, Regimentation, Unconstitutional," 1947, folder 14, FCP.

19. *Philadelphia Tribune*, Feb. 14, 1948, 1; clipping in file for Bernard Samuel, EBM.

20. *Philadelphia Tribune*, Feb. 14, 1948, 1, Feb. 24, 1948, 1, 3; clipping in file for Bernard Samuel, EBM; clipping from *Philadelphia Tribune*, Mar. 9, 1948, in folder F, box Research and Investigations Newspaper Clippings, clippings from *Philadelphia Evening Bulletin*, Feb. 19, 1948, *Philadelphia Afro-American*, Feb. 21, 1948, *Philadelphia Daily News*, Feb. 19, 1948, in scrapbook 1, box 21, JCRC; Graves, *Fair Employment Practice Legislation*, 214.

21. *Philadelphia Tribune*, Mar. 13, 1948, 1.

22. "First Annual Report of Philadelphia F.E.P. Commission," May 31, 1948, folder FEPC, box A418, Bernard Samuel Papers, City Archives; clippings from *Philadelphia*